I0102411

If

Violence
Has To Stop

Slaughterhouses
Must Close Down

By
Dr. Sahadeva dasa

B.com., FCA., AICWA., PhD
Chartered Accountant

Soul Science University Press

www.kindnessClub.org

Readers interested in the subject matter of this
book are invited to correspond with the publisher at:
SoulScienceUniversity@gmail.com   +91 98490 95990
or visit DrDasa.com

First Edition: November 2014

Soul Science University Press expresses its gratitude to the
Bhaktivedanta Book Trust International (BBT), for the use of quotes by
His Divine Grace A.C.Bhaktivedanta Swami Prabhupada.

ISBN 97893-82947-18-9

Published by:
Dr. Sahadeva dasa for Soul Science University Press

Printed by:
Rainbow Print Pack, Hyderabad

To order a copy write to purnabramhadasa@gmail.com
or buy online: Amazon.com, rlbdeshop.com

Dedicated to....

His Divine Grace A.C.Bhaktivedanta Swami Prabhupada

We want to stop these killing houses. It is very, very sinful. Therefore in Europe, so many wars. Every ten years, fifteen years, there is a big war and wholesale slaughter of the whole human kind. And these rascals, they do not see it. The reaction must be there. You are killing innocent cows and animals. Nature will take revenge. Wait for that. As soon as the time is ripe, the nature will gather all these rascals, and club, slaughter them. Finished. They will fight amongst themselves, Protestant and Catholic, Russia and France, and France and Germany. This is going on. Why? This is the nature's law. Tit for tat. You have killed. Now you get killed. Amongst yourselves. They are being sent to the slaughterhouse. And here, you'll create slaughterhouse, "Dum! dum!" and get killed.

~ Srila Prabhupada (Room Conversation -- June 11, 1974, Paris)

By The Same Author

Oil-Final Countdown To A Global Crisis And Its Solutions

End of Modern Civilization And Alternative Future

To Kill Cow Means To End Human Civilization

Cow And Humanity - Made For Each Other

Cows Are Cool - Love 'Em!

Let's Be Friends - A Curious, Calm Cow

Wondrous Glories of Vraja

We Feel Just Like You Do

Tsunami Of Diseases Headed Our Way - Know Your Food Before Time Runs Out

Cow Killing And Beef Export - The Master Plan To Turn India Into A Desert

Capitalism Communism And Cowism - A New Economics For The 21st `Century

Noble Cow - Munching Grass, Looking Curious And Just Hanging Around

World - Through The Eyes Of Scriptures

To Save Time Is To Lengthen Life

Life Is Nothing But Time - Time Is Life, Life Is Time

Lost Time Is Never Found Again

Spare Us Some Carcasses - An Appeal From The Vultures

An Inch of Time Can Not Be Bought With A Mile of Gold

Cow Dung For Food Security And Survival of Human Race

Cow Dung – A Down To Earth Solution To Global Warming And Climate Change

Career Women - The Violence of Modern Jobs And The Lost Art of Home Making

Working Moms And Rise of A Lost Generation

Glories of Thy Wondrous Name

India A World Leader in Cow Killing And Beef Export - An Italian Did It In 10 Years

As Long As There Are Slaughterhouses, There Will Be Wars

Peak Soil – Industrial Civilization, On The Verge of Eating Itself

Corporatocracy : The New Gods – Greedy, Ruthless And Reckless

(More information on availability on DrDasa.com)

Contents

Preface

1 We're Living In Violent Times   10

2 Violence And Types   17

3 There Must Be A Cause
For This Increased, Senseless Violence   20

4 Cruelty To Animals
Translates Into Crime Against Humanity   27

5 Eating Meat Is Animal Abuse   45

6 Meat Is Murder
Meat Eaters Have Blood On Their Hands   48

7 'Meat-Eaters Are Terrorists' - Chrissie Hynde   52

8 You Are Literally What You Eat
Slaughterhouse Products Are Imbued With Cruelty   57

9 "Can't Wait For Feeling You Get
When U Just Killed Some1"   62

10 Source Of Fascination
With The Head And Throat-Cutting   67

11 Use Of Child Soldiers In Conflicts
Rising Significantly   69

12 Some More Spine-chilling Statistics   71

13 Slaughterhouse Workers
More Likely To Be Violent   73

14 Killing For A Living
The Traumatic Consequences of Slaughterhouse Work   76

15 School Shooters Had Abused Animals First   87

16 All In The Fray - Woman, Kids And Grannies

    3 Year Olds To 90 Year Olds Join The War   90

17 Violence begets violence   97

18 Facts About Animal Abuse And Domestic Violence   99

19 Terror deaths 'jumped sharply in 2013'   102

20 Senseless Violence of A Desensitized Generation

    Baseball Player Killed By "Bored" Oklahoma Teens   105

21 Modern Conflicts: Dizzying Acts Of Brutality

    A Modern Mall Turns Into A Slaughterhouse   111

22 When An Animal Abuser

    Becomes A National Leader   114

23 Horrors of A Needless War

    A Young Woman's Heart-rending Appeal To Bomb Her   117

24 'Today There Is A Third World War'

    Pope Francis Condemns 'Piecemeal' World Of War   128

25 Dangerously Violent, Trigger-Happy Masses

    Woman Kills Three For Last X-Box at Chicago Wal-Mart   133

26 The Link Between Meat Production and Human Rights   137

27 The World In Need Of Real Civilization   157

28 "Do Unto Others ..."   159

29 How Can There Be Peace?   161

30 Time Has Come!

    March to Close All Slaughterhouses   164

    The Author

Preface

We are living in violent times and there is no disputing this fact. Wars are raging around the globe. There is war within the family, in the form of discontent, arguments, separation, and divorce; war in the community in the form of gang wars, crime, robberies, murders, and rape; there is internal war going on in almost half of the countries in the world. Then there are industrial and economic rivalries as well as international wars on terrorism.

This era of war is entering a new phase, in which the great divisions among humankind and the dominating source of international conflict will be cultural. Divisions between civilizations are deepening and increasing in importance. From Yugoslavia to the Middle East to Central Asia, the fault lines of civilizations are the battle lines of the future. Then there are weapons of mass destruction that can wipe out life in a matter of hours.

If you believe in the principle of cause and effect, there must be a cause for this senseless violence. We are becoming victims of war because we are raging a war on non-human life forms. What goes around comes around. As you sow so shall you reap. We are being slaughtered by sophisticated weaponry as we slaughter animals in state of the art slaughterhouses.

Plutarch offers an insight into the evolution of wars, "At the beginning it was some wild and harmful animal that was eaten, then a bird or fish that had its flesh torn. And so when our murderous instincts had tasted blood and grew practised on wild animals, they advanced to the labouring ox and the well-behaved sheep and the housewarding cock; thus, little by little giving a hard edge to our insatiable appetite, we have advanced to wars and the slaughter and murder of human beings."

According to author Cynthia Hodges, cruelty to animals and violence towards people have something in common: both types of victims are living beings, feel pain, experience distress, and may die from their injuries. Until recently, however, violence towards animals had been considered to be unrelated to violence towards children and the elderly, and other forms of violence. A correlation has now been established between animal abuse, family violence, and other forms of community violence. A growing body of research indicates that people who commit acts of cruelty towards animals rarely stop there.

It's time we realize this if we at all want a world which is safe for us and our children.

Sahadeva dasa

Dr. Sahadeva dasa
1st November 2014
Secunderabad, India

1

We're Living

In Violent Times

It is an accepted fact that modern civilization, in spite of all its technological and scientific progress, is morally deficient. Many inventions in the last 100 years have revolutionized the way we eat, sleep, work and communicate. But on many fronts we have failed and one of the most widely cited failings is that society is becoming more and more violent.

20th century has been the bloodiest century in all of human history. 20th century has witnessed, besides the two most brutal World Wars, the worst acts of barbarism — holocaust, Gulag Concentration camps, genocides and atomic bombing of Hiroshima and Nagasaki. And even since the close of the 20th century, we have incidents such as the September 11 attacks, countless suicide bombings, and more.

Growing up used to be less traumatic just a few decades ago. Children back then worried about such things as a flat tire on their bikes and hoped that their teacher wouldn't give too much homework.[1]

How life has changed. A 1994 poll found more than half the children questioned said they were afraid of violent crime against them or a family member. Are these kids just paranoid, or is there a real problem?

Well, it turns out this is not some irrational fear based upon a false perception of danger. Life has indeed become more violent and more dangerous for children. Consider the following statistics: One in six youths between the ages of 10 and 17 has seen or knows someone who has been shot. The estimated number of child abuse victims increased 40 percent between 1985 and 1991. Children under 18 were 244 percent more likely to be killed by guns in 1993 than they were in 1986. Violent crime has increased by more than 560 percent since 1960.[2]

The innocence of childhood has been replaced by the very real threat of violence. A child's exposure to violence is pervasive. Children see violence in their schools, their neighborhoods, and their homes. The daily news is rife with reports of child molestations and abductions. War in foreign lands along with daily reports of murder, rape, and robberies also heighten a child's perception of potential violence.[2]

Television in the home is the greatest source of visual violence for children. The average child watches 8,000 televised murders and 100,000 acts of violence before finishing elementary school. That number more than doubles by the time he or she reaches age 18.[3]

It's a scary world, and children are exposed to more violence than any generation in recent memory. An article in Newsweek magazine concluded: "It gets dark early in the Midwest this time of year. Long before many parents are home from work, the shadows creep up the walls and gather in the corners, while on the carpet a little figure sprawls in the glow emanating from an anchorman's tan. There's been a murder in the Loop, a fire in a nightclub, an indictment of another priest. Red and white lights swirl in urgent pinwheels as the ambulances howl down the dark streets. And one more crime that never gets reported, because there's no one to arrest. Who killed childhood? We all did."

Widespread Desensitization

We see violence all around us to such an extent that we are becoming immune to it. The wars that flare up in Congo and other

African states don't move us any more. In the Middle-East a number of bombs are detonated each month and it doesn't appear to affect us, despite the fact that thousands of people get murdered. Even so when we hear about it on the evening news, and all we seem to say is: "That is so terrible." Violence in our society is increasing, and we don't seem to mind it at all.[4]

No one minds even if a person is assaulted or murdered in broad daylight. No one steps in to help him or her. Nothing matters other than gross self-interest.

More Killed by Toddlers Than Terrorists in U.S

Americans hate terrorists and love kids, right? So you might be shocked to know that preschoolers (3-6 years old) with guns have taken more lives so far this year than the single U.S. terrorist attack, which claimed four lives in Boston.[5]

NSA spent billions on a spying program called PRISM but it would have saved more lives had it been monitoring toddlers – or gun owners – rather than suspected terrorists.

Did you know: So far this year, more Americans have been killed on U.S. soil by toddlers than terrorists.

In the first 5 months of 2013, there were 11 gun fatalities where a preschooler pulled the trigger whereas only 3 fatalities in a terrorist attack.

At least 10 more toddlers shot but not killed themselves or someone else during the same period. In the first three cases, the shooter was only 2 years old.

While this analysis focuses on children, another equally accurate headline could read:

U.S. Gun Violence Kills More Americans Than Terrorists Worldwide.

In 2010, 13,186 people died in terrorist attacks worldwide, while 31,672 people were killed with firearms in America alone, reports CNN's Samuel Burke.

More Americans Killed By Police Than By Terrorists or In International Wars

In the last decade, the number of people killed by US police has reached 5,000. The number of soldiers killed since the inception of the Iraq war, 4489. [6] An average American is 29 times more likely to be murdered by a cop than a terrorist! An "epidemic of police brutality" is sweeping this nation.

In several states like Utah, police officers have killed more civilians than gang members, drug dealers, or child abusers have over the past five years, according to a new report from the Salt Lake Tribune.[7]

A mass shooting happens every FIVE days in America:

Interactive map shows how gun violence is an epidemic sweeping the nation

The Brady Campaign to Prevent Gun Violence, a nonprofit lobbying group, has compiled an extensive list of the last 431 shootings with more than one victim since 2005, to create an elaborately detailed map that depicts the unimaginable scope of the senseless horrors.

The organization's data says that since 2005, there has been a multiple-victim shooting every 5.9 days in the United States, with

Americans are 8 times more likely to be killed by a police officer than by a terrorist.
-U.S. National Safety Council

87 people dying of bullet wounds each day.[8] The most dangerous city for mass shootings is Chicago.

A Virus of Violence

This virus of violence is occurring worldwide, and the explanation for it has to be some new factor that is occurring in all of these countries (Grossman, 1999b). Like heart disease, there are many factors involved in the causation of violent crime, and we must never downplay any of them.

Srila Prabhupada: Actually, I've seen in New York that in some quarters, it is so nasty. Disaster. So many storefronts and houses lying vacant. Just after my arrival there. I would sometimes walk to see various parts of the city. Hellish condition. People said it was risky, but [laughing] I did not know that it was risky.

One electrician who was my friend said. "Oh, Swamiji, you are going to that quarter? It is not for you. Don't."

"Oh, I do not care. What have I got that they could take from me?"

So I was going here and there in New York City. So many nasty quarters. London, also. So many houses vacant.

Disciple: Srila Prabhupada, some say there is more chance of being killed in New York City than in the jungle. Violent criminals are roaming the neighborhoods to rob and rape, because they know that very often, modern society isn't going to do much to stop them. These thugs can literally get away with murder.

Srila Prabhupada: Yes. People warned me not to go to Central Park in the evening. They said at night nobody goes there.

Disciple: That's quite true, Srila Prabhupada. At night ordinary people are afraid to go there. They have to stay inside, behind locked doors. Nobody can go to the park. Except the muggers and killers. They practically own the place.

Srila Prabhupada: Such an important park in such an important city, and no one can go there.

~ Srila Prabhupada (Conversation, New Vrindaban. West Virginia, June 26, 1976.)

First we must understand the magnitude of the problem. The murder rate does not accurately represent our situation. Murder has been held down by the development of ever more sophisticated life saving skills and techniques. A better indicator of the problem is the aggravated assault rate -- the rate at which human beings are attempting to kill one another. According to Interpol, between 1977 and 1993 the

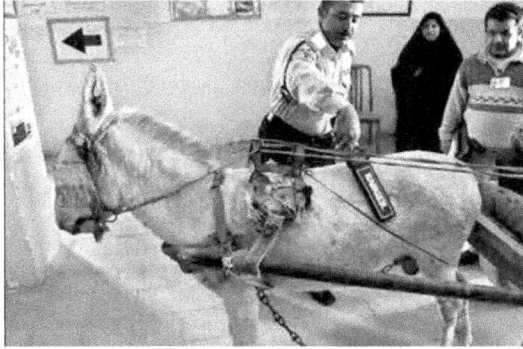

In the history of human race, there never has been so much distrust and unease. Neither has human race ever been so close to annihilation.

per capita assault rate increased nearly fivefold in Norway and Greece, and in Australia and New Zealand it increased approximately fourfold. During the same period it tripled in Sweden, and approximately doubled in: Belgium, Denmark, England-Wales, France, Hungary, Netherlands, and Scotland. In India during this period the per capita murder rate doubled. In Mexico and Brazil violent crime is also skyrocketing, and in Japan juvenile violent crime went up 30 percent in 1997 alone.[9]

In USA, it has gone up from around 60 per 100,000 in 1957, to over 440 per 100,000 by the mid-1990's (Statistical Abstracts of the United States, 1957-1997).

Reference

David H. Bailey, Isn't Society Becoming More And More Violent?, Violence in Society, 05 Oct 2014 (c) 2014

(1),(2),(3). Kerby Anderson, Violence In Society

(4). Increasing violence in our society, Dario.na

(5)Stacie Borrello, Tue, June 11, 2013, Opposing Views

(6) Matt Agorist, The Fee Thought Project, December 12, 2013

(7) German Lopez, November 24, 2014, Vox December 1, 2014

(8) Emily Anne Epstein, 27 July 2012, The Dailymail, UK

(9) Teaching Kids To Kill, Killology Research Group, ©2000 Warrior Science Group

2

Violence

And Types

The World Health Organization defines violence as "the intentional use of physical force or power, threatened or actual, against oneself, another person, or against a group or community, which either results in or has a high likelihood of resulting in injury, death, psychological harm, maldevelopment, or deprivation," but acknowledges that the inclusion of "the use of power" in its definition expands on the conventional meaning of the word.[1] This definition associates intentionality with the committing of the act itself, irrespective of the outcome it produces. Generally, though, anything that is turbulent or excited in an injurious, damaging or destructive way, or presenting risk accordingly, may be described as violent or occurring violently, even if not signifying violence (by a person and against a person).

Globally, violence takes the lives of more than 1.6 million people annually. Just over 50% due to suicide, some 35% due to homicide, and just over 12% as a direct result of war or some other form of conflict. In Africa, out of every 100,000 people, each year an estimated 60.9 die a violent death.[2] Statistics show that gunfire kills ten children a day in the United States. Corlin, past president of the American Medical Association said: "The United States leads the world—in

17

the rate at which its children die from firearms." He concluded,
"Gun violence is a threat to the public health of our country."[3] For each single death due to violence, there are dozens of hospitalizations, hundreds of emergency department visits, and thousands of doctors' appointments.[4] Furthermore, violence often has lifelong consequences for victims' physical and mental health and social functioning and can slow economic and social development.

Violence is a choice, and it is preventable.

Broadly divided, there are nine distinct forms of violence and abuse:

1. Physical Violence

Physical violence occurs when someone uses a part of their body or an object to control a person's actions.

2. Sexual Violence

Sexual violence occurs when a person is forced to unwillingly take part in sexual activity.

3. Emotional Violence

Emotional violence occurs when someone says or does something to make a person feel stupid or worthless.

4. Psychological Violence

Psychological violence occurs when someone uses threats and causes fear in an individual to gain control.

5. Spiritual Violence

Spiritual (or religious) violence occurs when someone uses an individual's spiritual beliefs to manipulate, dominate or control that person.

6. Cultural Violence

Cultural violence occurs when an individual is harmed as a result of practices that are part of her or his culture, religion or tradition.

7. Verbal Abuse

Verbal abuse occurs when someone uses language, whether spoken or written, to cause harm to an individual.

8. Financial Abuse

Financial abuse occurs when someone controls an individual's financial resources without the person's consent or misuses those resources.

9. Neglect

Neglect occurs when someone has the responsibility to provide care or assistance for an individual but does not.

Reference:

[1]Wikipedia, Krug et al., "World report on violence and health", World Health Organization, 2002.

[2} Awake Aug 8/05 pp. 4-7

[3} Awake Jul 8/2003 pp. 5-9

[4} "Global Burden of Disease", World Health Organization, 2008.

WHO / Liverpool JMU Centre for Public Health, "Violence Prevention: The evidence"

3

There Must Be A Cause

For This Increased, Senseless Violence

If you believe in the principle of cause and effect, there must be a cause for this increased, senseless violence. The Principle of Cause and Effect describes the philosophical concept of causality, stating that every event is an effect and has another event as a cause and is itself the cause of yet another effect. The principle also maintains that there is no such thing as chance as an uncaused happening. Whatever happens, there must be a cause for it, nothing comes from nothing. If we cannot see a cause for an event it does not mean there is none - it merely means that the cause is obscure and not known.[1]

For thousands of years, the law of cause and effect guided scientific inquiry. In fact, the history of the concept of causality can be traced through Vedic, Hebrew, Babylonian, Greek and European cultures. Certain Greek philosophers, however, introduced the atomistic concept of chance-events to oppose the common-sense application of causality. The resulting conflict between cause versus chance has not only shaped the history of science but has imposed lasting effects on Western culture as a whole. This conflict intensified during the Twentieth Century as the Heisenberg Uncertainty Principle (HUP) became the leading tool of the proponents of chance. More recent findings have now demonstrated that the HUP fails in six actual cases. Common Sense Science counters chance-based philosophy by returning to causality and other principles of Classical Science such as the conservation of energy and the use of physical finite-sized models for fundamental particles (e.g., the electron).[2]

The Law of Cause and Effect states that every material effect must have an adequate antecedent or simultaneous cause. The mass of a paper clip is not going to provide sufficient gravitational pull to cause a tidal wave. There must be an adequate cause for the tidal wave, like a massive, offshore, underwater earthquake. Leaning against a mountain will certainly not cause it to topple over. Jumping up and down on the ground will not cause an earthquake. If a chair is not placed in an empty room, the room will remain chairless. If matter was not made and placed in the Universe, we would not exist. There must be an adequate antecedent or simultaneous cause for every material effect. Perhaps the Law of Cause and Effect seems intuitive to most, but common sense is foreign to many when it is brought into the discussion.[3]

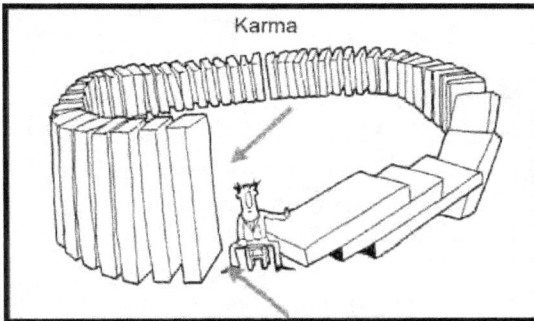

In Sanskrit, this principle of cause and effect is known as karma. In Bible it is described as, 'As you sow, so shall you reap'. This principle governs every aspect of our life and rewards our every deed, however big or small.

In the context of modern day violence, we can remember the saying, 'The fate of the animals and the fate of man are interconnected.' (Ecclesiastes 3:19) A.C. Bhaktivedanta Swami Prabhupada said in 1974:

"We simply request, 'Don't kill. Don't maintain slaughterhouses.' That is very sinful. It brings a very awkward karmic reaction upon society. Stop these slaughterhouses. We don't say, 'Stop eating meat.' You can eat meat, but don't take it from the slaughterhouse, by killing. Simply wait (until the animal dies of natural causes) and you'll get the carcasses.

"You are killing innocent cows and other animals--nature will take revenge. Just wait. As soon as the time is right, nature will gather all these rascals and slaughter them. Finished. They'll fight among themselves--Protestants and Catholics, Russia and America, this one and that one. It is going on. Why? This is nature's law. Tit for tat. 'You have killed. Now you kill yourselves.'

"They are sending animals to the slaughterhouse, and now they'll create their own slaughterhouse. You see? Just take Belfast. The Roman Catholics are killing the Protestants, and the Protestants are killing the Catholics. This is nature's law. It is not necessary that you be sent to the ordinary slaughterhouse. You'll make a slaughterhouse at home. You'll kill your own child--abortion. This is nature's law.

"Who are these children being killed? They are these meat-eaters. They enjoyed themselves when so many animals were killed and now they're being killed by their own mothers. People do not know how nature is working. If you kill you must be killed. If you kill the cow, who is your mother, then in some future lifetime your mother will kill you. Yes. The mother becomes the child, and the child becomes the mother.

"We don't want to stop trade, or the production of grains and vegetables and fruit. But we want to stop these killing houses. It is very, very sinful. That is why all over the world they have so many wars. Every ten or fifteen years there is a big war--a wholesale slaughterhouse for humankind. But these rascals--they do not see it, that by the law of karma, every action must have its reaction."

As long as man continues to be the ruthless destroyer of lower living beings he will never know health or peace. For as long as men massacre animals, they will kill each other. Indeed, he who sows the seed of murder and pain cannot reap joy and love. - Ovid

Similarly, in his purport to the Srimad Bhagavatam 6.10.9, Srila Prabhupada writes: "One cannot continue killing animals and at the same time be a religious man. That is the greatest hypocrisy. Jesus Christ said, 'Do not kill,' but hypocrites nevertheless maintain thousands of slaughterhouses while posing as Christians. Such hypocrisy is condemned..."

And:

"If one kills many thousands of animals in a professional way so that other people can purchase the meat to eat, one must be ready to be killed in a similar way in his next life and in life after life. There are many rascals who violate their own religious principles. According to Judeo-Christian scriptures, it is clearly said, 'Thou shalt not kill.' Nonetheless, giving all kinds of excuses, even the heads of religions indulge in killing animals while trying to pass as saintly persons. This mockery and hypocrisy in human society brings about unlimited calamities; therefore occasionally there are great wars. Masses of such people go out onto battlefields and kill themselves. Presently, they have discovered the atomic bomb, which is simply waiting to be used for wholesale destruction." (Chaitanya Charitamrita, Madhya 24.251, purport)

Also:

"To be nonviolent to human beings and to be a killer or enemy of the poor animals is Satan's philosophy. In this age there is enmity towards poor animals, and therefore the poor creatures are always anxious. The reaction of the poor animals is being forced on human society, and therefore there is always the strain of cold or hot war between men, individually, collectively or nationally."

(Srimad Bhagavatam 1.10.6, purport)

"In human society, if one kills a man he has to be hanged. That is the law of the state. Because of ignorance people do not perceive that there is a complete state controlled by the Supreme Lord. Every living creature is the son of the Supreme Lord, and He does not tolerate even an ant's being killed. One has to pay for it."

In his 1987 booklet, The New Abolitionists: Animal Rights and Human Liberation, subtitled, "An introduction to the ascendant animal rights movement, framed in the historical context of human emancipation and explained in the terminology of progressive thought and politics," B.R. Boyd similarly writes:

"With more and more people sensing connections between the looming global violence of environmental collapse and thermonuclear war, on the one hand, and our various 'localized' or specific violences of child abuse, sexual assault, class exploitation, etc., on the other, the message of the animal rights movement echoes an ancient Chinese Buddhist saying:

"If you wish to know

"Why there are disasters

"Of armies and weapons in the world

"Listen to the piteous cries

"From the slaughterhouse at midnight"

"Whether viewed spiritually as karma or in secular, psychological terms as the natural result of our individual and collective psychic numbing to the suffering we inflict, it does seem that our violence comes back to haunt us -- as we have sown, so are we reaping -- and that the roots of our ecological and nuclear dilemma reach deep into our history and our psychology."

"It seems increasingly clear that a thoroughgoing solution to the big problems we face will require a radical change in many of our ways of thinking and feeling and being in the world. Radical ecofeminism and some other wholistic perspectives are teaching us that an integral part of that change lies in learning to balance our intellect -- including clear-headed analysis, which is essential -- with our emotions, integrating head and heart, and developing circular and complete relationships with the earth and her creatures, as contrasted with the separated, linear patterns and the absolute primacy of intellect over feeling and intuition that seem to typify Western patriarchal thinking."

Pythagoras warned: "Those who kill animals for food will be more prone than vegetarians to torture and kill their fellow men."

"When we turn to the protection of animals, we sometimes hear it said that we ought to protect men first and animals afterwards...By condoning cruelty to animals, we perpetuate the very spirit which condones cruelty to men." --Henry Salt

George T. Angell, founder of the Massachusetts Society for the Prevention of Cruelty to Animals, said, "I am sometimes asked, 'Why do you spend time and money talking about kindness to animals when there is cruelty to men?' I answer: 'I am working at the roots.'"

"The vegetarian movement," wrote Count Leo Tolstoy, "ought to fill with gladness the souls of all those who have at their heart the realization of God's Kingdom on earth."

Enjoy Karma

In a 1979 essay entitled "Abortion and the Language of Unconsciousness," contemporary spiritual leader Ravindra-svarupa dasa explains Srila Prabhupada's words in terms of a secular slippery slope argument, familiar to pro-lifers:

"A (spiritually) conscious person will not kill even animals (much less very young humans) for his pleasure or convenience. Certainly the unconsciousness and brutality that allows us to erect factories of death for animals lay the groundwork for our treating humans in the same way."

Animals are like children. If you can't see toddlers as persons, how will you ever see zygotes and embryos as persons?

In the April 1995 issue of Harmony: Voices for a Just Future, a peace and justice periodical on the religious left, Catholic civil rights activist Bernard Broussard similarly concludes:

"...our definition of war is much too limited and narrow. Wars and conflicts in the human kingdom will never be abolished or diminished until, as a pure matter of logic, it includes the cessation of war between the human and animal kingdoms.

"For, if we be eaters of flesh, or wearers of fur, or participants in hunting animals, or in any way use our might against weakness, we are promoting, in no matter how seemingly insignificant a fashion, the spirit of war."'

The "might makes right" mentality that makes abortion possible begins with what we humans do to other animals.

Reference

(1) Seven Hermetic Principles, Raven's Tarrots.

(2) David L. Bergman and Glen C. Collins, The Law of Cause and Effect, Dominant Principle of Classical Physics.

(3) Jeff Miller, Ph.D., God and the Laws of Science: The Law of Causality

4

Cruelty To Animals

Translates Into Crime Against Humanity

According to author Cynthia Hodges, cruelty to animals and violence towards people have something in common: both types of victims are living beings, feel pain, experience distress, and may die from their injuries. [1] Until recently, however, violence towards animals had been considered to be unrelated to violence towards children and the elderly, and other forms of domestic violence. [2] A correlation has now been established between animal abuse, family violence, and other forms of community violence. [3] A growing body of research indicates that people who commit acts of cruelty towards animals rarely stop there. [4] Murderers and people who abuse their spouse or children had frequently harmed animals

> *"At the beginning it was some wild and harmful animal that was eaten, then a bird or fish that had its flesh torn. And so when our murderous instincts had tasted blood and grew practised on wild animals, they advanced to the labouring ox and the well-behaved sheep and the housewarding cock; thus, little by little giving a hard edge to our insatiable appetite, we have advanced to wars and the slaughter and murder of human beings."*
> *~ Plutarch*

in the past. [5] People who abuse animals may also be dangerous to people. [6]

Child and animal protection professionals are aware of this connection, and recognize that both child and animal abuse are linked in a self-perpetuating cycle of violence. [7] One reason for this is that individuals who witness abuse or other violence become desensitized to it. Research shows that the more often someone is exposed to a certain situation, the more comfortable that person becomes with it.[8] Criminal psychologists acknowledge that participating in or viewing acts of repeated cruelty towards animals desensitizes both the perpetrator and the spectator. [9] John Locke once wrote of children that "...tormenting and killing...beasts, will, by degrees, harden their minds even towards men; and they who delight in the suffering and destruction of inferior creatures, will not be apt to be very compassionate or benign to those of their own

The demoniac are engaged in activities that will lead the world to destruction. The Lord states here that they are less intelligent The materialists, who have no concept of God, think that they are advancing. But according to Bhagavad-gita, they are unintelligent and devoid of all sense. They try to enjoy this material world to the utmost limit and therefore always engage in inventing something for sense gratification. Such materialistic inventions are considered to be advancement of human civilization, but the result is that people grow more and more violent and more and more cruel -- cruel to animals and cruel to other human beings. They have no idea how to behave toward one another. Animal killing is very prominent amongst demoniac people. Such people are considered the enemies of the world, because ultimately they will invent or create something which will bring destruction to all. Indirectly, this verse anticipates the invention of nuclear weapons, of which the whole world is today very proud. At any moment war may take place, and these atomic weapons may create havoc. Such things are created solely for the destruction of the world, and this is indicated here. Due to godlessness, such weapons are invented in human society; they are not meant for the peace and prosperity of the world."

~ Srila Prabhupada (Bhagavad-gita 16.9)

kind." [10] Animal cruelty destroys respect for life, [11] and children who witness animal abuse are at a greater risk of becoming abusers themselves. [12]

Animal Abuse As A Predictor Of Future Behavior

Cruelty to animals can be a warning sign of future violent behavior. [13] A child's aggressive, abusive behavior towards animals may predict later violence towards people. [14] Child protection and social service agencies, mental health professionals, and educators regard animal abuse as a significant form of aggressive and antisocial behavior, and consider it to be an important red flag in identifying other violent behavior. [15] A child's aggressive, abusive behavior towards animals may predict later violence towards people.

Children and adolescents may abuse animals out of curiosity or exploration, peer pressure, mood enhancement (i.e., to relieve boredom or depression), as a way to emotionally abuse others, or as practice for future interpersonal violence. [16] In addition, adults may commit acts of cruelty to animals in order to express aggression

I have found that since I have stopped eating meat, I've become less angry and aggressive. Before entering this diet, I did eat organic chicken and turkey. So I wasn't ingesting any steroids, etc.
It's amazing how much lighter and better I feel.
~ James Carpenter, March 21, 2011

through an animal (i.e., train an animal to attack by using pain to create a "mean" dog), enhance one's own aggressiveness (e.g., use an animal victim for target practice), or to satisfy sadistic urges (i.e., to enjoy the suffering experienced by the animal victim). [17]

There is a significant correlation between acts of cruelty to animals as a child and serious, recurrent aggression towards people as an adult. [18] In fact, one of the most reliable predictors of future violence as an adult is having committed animal abuse as a child. [19] Research in psychology and criminology indicates that people who commit acts of cruelty to animals often do not stop there — many of them later turn on humans. [20] Psychology, sociology, and criminology studies have shown that many violent offenders had committed repeated acts of serious animal cruelty during childhood and adolescence. [21] People who abused pets as children are more likely to commit murder or other violent crimes as adults. [22] In fact, violent criminals are five times more likely to commit violent crimes against people if they did so against animals as youths. [23] There is a further correlation: the most aggressive criminals had committed the most severe acts of animal cruelty in childhood. [24]

Acts of animal cruelty are not merely signs of a minor personality flaw, but are rather symptomatic of a deep mental disturbance.

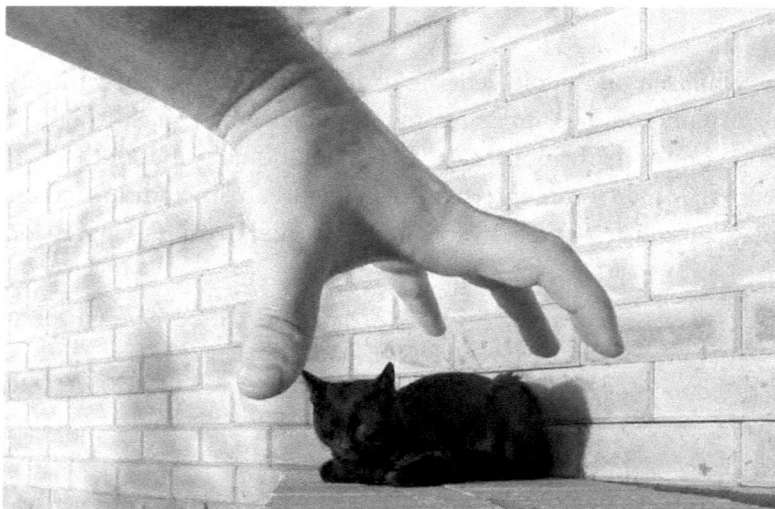

[25] Cruelty to animals has been recognized as an indicator of a dangerous psychopathy that claims both animal and human victims. [26] A survey of psychiatric patients who had repeatedly tortured animals found that all of them were also highly aggressive towards people. [27]

Acts of violence beget acts of increased violence. [28] It is a matter of escalation: people who want to victimize start with something they can easily control, then they work their way up. [29] A person who only feels powerful and in control while inflicting pain or death must continually sustain that "high" by committing acts that are more heinous or morbid. [30] The violent act itself must be viewed as dangerous, without regard as to whether the victim is a person or an animal. [31] An example of this escalation is the "Vampire cult leader," Rod Ferrell, who is serving a life sentence for bludgeoning a Florida couple to death. [32] Ferrell first drew the attention of law enforcement in Kentucky, where he was charged with breaking into an animal shelter where two puppies were tortured, killed and mutilated. [33]

Say No to violence. Respect Life.

The link between animal abuse and violence towards people is supported by studies, which have shown that:

100% of sexual homicide offenders examined had a history of cruelty towards animals. [34]

70% of all animal abusers have committed at least one other criminal offense and almost 40% have committed violent crimes against people. [35]

63.3% of men who had committed crimes of aggression admitted to cruelty to animals. [36]

48% of rapists and 30% of child molesters reported committing animal abuse during childhood or adolescence. [37]

36% of assaultive women reported cruelty to animals while 0% of non-assaultive women did. [38]

25% of violent, incarcerated men reported higher rates of "substantial cruelty to animals" in childhood than a comparison group of non-incarcerated men (0%). [39]

Men who abused animals were five times more likely to have been arrested for violence towards humans, four times more likely to have committed property crimes, and three times more likely to have records for drug and disorderly conduct offenses. [40]

Serial Killers

Researchers consider a fascination with cruelty to animals as a red flag that may indicate that a person is a serial killer or rapist.[41] According to the deputy manager of animal cruelty issues for the Humane Society of the United States, Dale Bartlett, "...the research shows that most mass murderers and serial killers are likely to have animal cruelty in their background." [42]

The Federal Bureau of Investigation (FBI) considers past animal abuse when profiling serial killers.[43] According to Robert K. Ressler, who developed profiles of serial killers for the FBI, "Murderers... very often start out by killing and torturing animals as kids."[44] FBI criminal profiler, John Douglas, writes in The Mind Hunter that serial offenders' earliest acts of violence are often the torture and/or killing of pets or wildlife, then brutalizing younger siblings, and then finally engaging in domestic violence or street crime. [45]

History is replete with serial killers whose violent tendencies were first directed towards animals. [46] Mass murderers Ted Bundy, Jeffrey Dahmer, Albert DeSalvo, and others committed heinous acts of animal cruelty before brutally killing their human victims. [47] Jeffrey Dahmer's first victims were animals: he decapitated dogs and staked cats to trees in his youth. [48] He also impaled frogs, cats, and dogs' heads on sticks. [49] Albert DeSalvo, the "Boston Strangler," who was convicted of killing 13 women, trapped dogs and cats and shot arrows at them through boxes as a youth. [50] Dennis Rader, the "BTK" killer, wrote in a chronological account of his childhood about hanging a dog and a cat. [51] Convicted sniper, Lee Boyd Malvo, who killed 10 people, had "pelted—and probably killed—numerous cats with marbles from a slingshot when he was about 14." [52] Ted Bundy also tortured his pets as a child. [53]

School Shooters

The deadly violence that has occurred in schools in recent years has, in most cases, begun with cruelty to animals. [54] Many of the school shooters committed acts of animal cruelty before turning their aggression on classmates, teachers, and parents. [55]

Eric Harris and Dylan Klebold, who shot and killed 12 students at Columbine High School, spoke of mutilating animals to their classmates. [56] Luke Woodham, who murdered his mother and two schoolmates, tortured and killed his own pet dog beforehand. [57] He wrote in his journal about setting Sparkle on fire, [58] describing

her dying howls as a "thing of beauty." [59] High-school killer, Kip Kinkel, tortured animals before going on his shooting spree. [60] He was reported to have blown up cows and decapitated cats. [61] Andrew Golden is said to have shot dogs, even his own pet dog, with a .22 caliber rifle before attacking his classmates. [62]

Animal Abuse As An Indicator Of Domestic Violence Or Neglect

In recent years, a strong connection has been made between animal abuse and domestic violence. [63] In fact, cruelty to animals is considered to be a significant predictor of future domestic violence. [64] According to Phil Arkow, humane educator and chair of the Latham Foundation's Child and Family Violence Prevention Project, "[f]amily violence often begins with pet abuse." [65] When animals in a home are abused or neglected, it is a warning sign that others in the household may not be safe. [66] Because abusers target the powerless, crimes against animals, spouses, children, and the elderly often go hand in hand. [67] Researchers have found that a batterer's first target is often an animal living in the home, while the second is a spouse or a child. [68]

Parents who neglect or abuse animals may also abuse or neglect their own children. [69] For example, Indiana residents Jade M. Jonas and Michael R. Smith faced felony charges when authorities discovered their two children and three dogs languishing in their filthy house. [70] According to news sources, officials first found a tethered dog deprived of food and water outside the home. [71] Upon entering the couple's residence, investigators found a 3-month-old boy lying near piles of feces, trash, and rotten food. [72] There was also a half-clothed toddler and two other dogs. [73] In another case, Illinois authorities found 40 parasite-ridden dogs amid 6 inches of feces on property occupied by John Morris. [74] Officials responding to neighbors' concerns found the sick and emaciated dogs confined to filthy animal carriers before discovering three children living in similar conditions. [75]

Abusive family members may threaten, injure, or kill pets as a way of controlling others in the family. [76] According to Susan Urban, a certified social worker with the ASPCA's Counseling Services, "in domestic violence,... the perpetrator often uses the animal to hurt a particular person - usually the person who loves and cares for the pet. The animal is abused in order to intimidate, harass or silence the vulnerable person." [77] The message the perpetrator is sending is, "Look what I can do to your animal, and imagine what I can do to you." [78] In addition, the perpetrator may retaliate against a person by hurting his or her pets or by otherwise abusing animals in that person's presence. [79] Studies have found that from 54 to 71 percent of women seeking shelter report that their partners had threatened, injured or killed one or more family pets. [80]

When a family member abuses an elderly relative's pet, the motivations may be complex. [81] Many older adults are particularly attached to their pets, which makes their pets vulnerable to abuse by those who want to exert power and control over the elderly person. [82] The perpetrator may neglect or abuse an elderly person's pet as a form of control or retaliation, out of frustration over their care-taking responsibilities, or as a way to extract financial assets. [83]

In cases of child abuse, perpetrators often abuse animals to exert their power and control over children and other vulnerable family members. [84] In some cases, abusers will force children to sexually abuse, hurt, or kill a pet. [85] Threats of animal abuse may also be used to intimidate children to keep silent about being victims of abuse. [86]

To summarize, batterers may threaten, abuse, or kill animals to Demonstrate and confirm power and control over the family; [87]

Isolate the victim and children; [88]

Eliminate competition for attention; [89]

Force the family to keep violence a secret; [90]

Teach submission; [91]

Retaliate for acts of independence and self-determination; [92]

Perpetuate terror; [93]

Prevent the victim from leaving or coerce him or her to return; [94]

Punish the victim for leaving; [95] or to

Since I suffer when pinched or killed by others, I should not attempt to pinch or kill any other living entity. People do not know that because of killing innocent animals they themselves will have to suffer severe reactions from material nature. Any country where people indulge in unnecessary killing of animals will have to suffer from wars and pestilence imposed by material nature. Comparing one's own suffering to the suffering of others, therefore, one should be kind to all living entities.

—Srila Prabhupada (Srimad Bhagavatam 7.15.24)

Degrade the victim through involvement in the abuse. [96]

Witnessing abuse towards parents or pets may compromise a child's psychological adjustment, increase his propensity for interpersonal violence, and make children's cruelty to animals more likely to emerge as a symptom of distress. [97] Children who have witnessed domestic violence or who have been the victims of physical or sexual abuse may also become animal abusers themselves,

imitating the violence they have seen or experienced. [98]

Children who abuse animals may be repeating a lesson learned at home, [99] engaging in post-traumatic reenactment of a violent episode, [100] or may be reacting to anger or frustration with violence. [101] Researchers say that a child's violence towards animals often represents displaced hostility and aggression stemming from neglect or abuse of the child or of another family member. [102] Some children may express the pain of victimization by abusing vulnerable family pets. [103] A victimized child may try to regain a sense of power by victimizing a more vulnerable animal. [104] Children in violent homes frequently participate in this pecking-order battery, in which they may injure or kill an animal. [105]

The correlation between domestic violence and animal abuse is supported by studies, which have shown that:

88% of 57 New Jersey families in which child abuse occurred also had incidents of animal abuse; [106]

85% of women and 63% of children entering shelters discussed incidents of pet abuse in the family; [107]

More than 80% of families being treated for child abuse were also involved in animal abuse; [108]

70.3% of women in domestic abuse shelters reported either threats or actual harm to pets, with 54% reporting actual harm; [109]

60% of families with child abuse and neglect also had pets that were abused or neglected; [110]

32% of pet-owning victims of domestic abuse reported that one or more of their children had hurt or killed a pet; [111]

Approximately 25% of the battered women reported that concern for their pets' welfare had prevented them from seeking shelter sooner; [112] and

12% of the reported intentional animal cruelty cases also involved some form of family violence, including domestic violence, child abuse, spouse/child witnessing animal cruelty, or elder abuse. [113]

Abuse Of Any Living Being Is Unacceptable And Endangers Everyone

Courts should aggressively penalize animal abusers, examine families for other signs of violence, and order perpetrators to undergo

psychological evaluations and counseling. [114] The deputy manager of animal cruelty issues for the Humane Society of the United States, Dale Bartlett, says that they "are trying to impress upon the courts and prosecutors, who handle cases of murder and rape, and often do not take animal abuse seriously that they must begin to realize the connection between how abusers treat people and animals." [115] Schools, parents, communities, and courts that dismiss cruelty to animals as a "minor" crime are ignoring a time bomb. [116]

According to Phil Arkow, humane educator and chair of the Latham Foundation's Child and Family Violence Prevention Project, "Animal abuse must be redefined as a crime of violence..."

and "it must be perceived and documented as a human welfare issue." [117] Judy Priess of the SASA Crisis Center says a connection needs to be established "that hurting an animal is just as bad as hurting a person." [118] She believes that if one can prevent a person from abusing animals as an adolescent, one can stop him from abusing people as an adult. [119]

Communities must acknowledge that the abuse of any living being is unacceptable and endangers everyone . [120] Recognizing that cruelty to animals is a significant form of aggressive and antisocial behavior may help further the understanding and prevention of violence. [121]

Source:

Cynthia Hodges, The Link: Cruelty to Animals and Violance Towards People, Michigan State University College of Law, 2008

[1] Animal Abuse and Violent Offending , Juvenile Justice Bulletin (September 2001), at http://www.ncjrs.gov/html/ojjdp/jjbul2001_9_2/page4.html (last visited June 27, 2007).

[2] The Animal Abuse-Human Violence Link , Progressive Animal Welfare Society, at http://www.paws.org/help/report/connection.php (last visited June 27, 2007).

[3] Understanding the Link® between violence to people and animals , American Humane Association, at http://www.americanhumane.org/site/PageServer?pagename=nr_fact_sheets_link (last visited June 27, 2007).

[4] The Animal Abuse-Human Violence Link, at http://www.paws.org/help/report/connection.php .

[5] Animal Alternatives in Education: The Link Between Human Violence and Animal Cruelty , The National Anti-Vivisection Society, at http://www.navs.org/site/PageServer?pagename=ain_edu_link_violence_cruelty (last visited July 3, 2007).

[6] Animal Abuse and Violent Offending, at http://www.ncjrs.gov/html/ojjdp/jjbul2001_9_2/page5.html .

[7] Understanding the Link® between violence to people and animals , at http://www.americanhumane.org/site/PageServer?pagename=nr_fact_sheets_link.

[8] Animal Alternatives in Education: The Link Between Human Violence and Animal Cruelty, at http://www.navs.org/site/PageServer?pagename=ain_edu_link_violence_cruelty .

[9] Phyllis M. Daugherty, Animal abusers may be warming up for more (February 24, 2005), at http://www.lacp.org/2005-Articles-Main/LAPDsDedicatedAnimalCrueltyUnit. html (last visited June 27, 2007).

[10] Modern History Sourcebook: John Locke (1632-1704), Some Thoughts Concerning Education , 1692 , at http://www.fordham.edu/halsall/mod/1692locke-education.html (last visited June 27, 2007).

[11] Irwin Feldman, Where Violence Begins: Animal Industries and the Cult of Aggression , at http://www.animalsvoice.com/PAGES/writes/editorial/essays/hunting/ feldman_violence.html (last visited June 27, 2007).

[12] Understanding the Link® between violence to people and animals , at http:// www.americanhumane.org/site/PageServer?pagename=nr_fact_sheets_link .

[13] The Animal Abuse-Human Violence Link, at http://www.paws.org/help/report/ connection.php .

[14] If Your Kid is Torturing Animals, We've All Got a Problem, The Desert Sun (April 2005), at http://www.animalsvoice.com/PAGES/writes/editorial/news/comment/ kid_torturing.html (last visited June 29, 2007).

[15] The Animal Abuse-Human Violence Link, at http://www.paws.org/help/ report/connection.php .

[16] Animal Abuse and Violent Offending, at http://www.ncjrs.gov/html/ojjdp/ jjbul2001_9_2/page6.html .

[17] Id.

[18] Mary Lou Randour, What We Know About the Link Between Animal Abuse and Human Violence , at http://www.animalsvoice.com/PAGES/writes/editorial/ features/link/randour_link.html (last visited June 29, 2007).

[19] Holly Nash, DVM, MS, Animal Cruelty/Human Violence: The Link , at http:// www.peteducation.com/article.cfm?cls=0&cat=1495&articleid=3120 (last visited June 27, 2007).

[20] Animal Abuse and Human Abuse: Partners in Crime , People for the Ethical Treatment of Animals, at http://www.helpinganimals.com/Factsheet/files/ FactsheetDisplay.asp?ID=18 (last visited June 27, 2007)..

[21] Susan I. Finkelstein , Canary in a Coal Mine: The Connection Between Animal Abuse and Human Violence , Penn Veterinary Medicine, at http://www.vet.upenn. edu/schoolresources/communications/publications/bellwether/58/connection.html (last visited June 27, 2007).

[22] Animal Cruelty/Human Violence: The Link, at http://www.peteducation.com/ article.cfm?cls=0&cat=1495&articleid=3120 .

[23] Robert Price, Cruelty to animals may lead to child abuse , KHAS-TV, at http:// khastv.com/modules/news/article.php?storyid=9304 (last visited June 27, 2007).

[24] Randour, What We Know About the Link , Between Animal Abuse and Human Violence , at. http://www.animalsvoice.com/PAGES/writes/editorial/features/link/randour_link.html .

[25] Animal Abuse and Human Abuse: Partners in Crime, at http://www.helpinganimals.com/Factsheet/files/FactsheetDisplay.asp?ID=18 .

[26] Id .

[27] Id .

[28] Daugherty, Animal abusers may be warming up for more , at http://www.lacp.org/2005-Articles-Main/LAPDsDedicatedAnimalCrueltyUnit.html .

[29] Criminologists find link between animal cruelty, later violence, Associated Press (March 2, 2004), at http://www.animalsvoice.com/PAGES/writes/editorial/news/invest/AP_link.html (last viewed June 29, 2007).

[30] Daugherty, Animal abusers may be warming up for more , at http://www.lacp.org/2005-Articles-Main/LAPDsDedicatedAnimalCrueltyUnit.html .

[31] Richard Weizel, Animal abuse predictor of domestic violence , Connecticut Post Online, at http://www.chronicleforums.com/Forum/showthread.php?p=2448275#post2448275 (originally at http://www.connpost.com/localnews/ci_5942231) (last visited June 27, 2007).

[32] Id .

[33] Id .

[34] Animal Abuse and Human Abuse: Partners in Crime, at http://www.helpinganimals.com/Factsheet/files/FactsheetDisplay.asp?ID=18 .

[35] The Animal Abuse-Human Violence Link, at http://www.paws.org/help/report/connection.php .

[36] Animal Abuse and Violent Offending, at http://www.ncjrs.gov/html/ojjdp/jjbul2001_9_2/page4.html .

[37] Id .

[38] Id.

[39] Id.

[40] Randour, What We Know About the Link , Between Animal Abuse and Human Violence , at. http://www.animalsvoice.com/PAGES/writes/editorial/features/link/randour_link.html .

[41] Animal Abuse and Human Abuse: Partners in Crime, at http://www.helpinganimals.com/Factsheet/files/FactsheetDisplay.asp?ID=18 .

[42] Weizel, Animal abuse predictor of domestic violence , at http://www.chronicleforums.com/Forum/showthread.php?p=2448275#post2448275 .

[43] The Animal Abuse-Human Violence Link, at http://www.paws.org/help/report/connection.php .

[44]   Animal Abuse and Human Abuse: Partners in Crime, at http://www.helpinganimals.com/Factsheet/files/FactsheetDisplay.asp?ID=18 .

[45] Daugherty, Animal abusers may be warming up for more , at http://www.lacp.org/2005-Articles-Main/LAPDsDedicatedAnimalCrueltyUnit.html .

[46]   Animal Abuse and Human Abuse: Partners in Crime, at http://www.helpinganimals.com/Factsheet/files/FactsheetDisplay.asp?ID=18 .

[47]   Animal abuse predictor of domestic violence , at http://www.chronicleforums.com/Forum/showthread.php?p=2448275#post2448275.

[48] Why You Should Join The War On Animal Cruelty , Coalition for Animal Justice, at http://www.animal-justice.org/involved.html (last viewed at June 29, 2007).

[49] Animal Abuse and Human Abuse: Partners in Crime, at http://www.helpinganimals.com/Factsheet/files/FactsheetDisplay.asp?ID=18 .

[50] Id .

[51] Id .

[52] Id.

[53] Why You Should Join The War On Animal Cruelty , at http://www.animal-justice.org/involved.html .

[54] Id .

[55] Randour, What We Know About the Link Between Animal Abuse and Human Violence, at http://www.animalsvoice.com/PAGES/writes/editorial/features/link/randour_link.html .

[56]   Animal Abuse and Human Abuse: Partners in Crime, at http://www.helpinganimals.com/Factsheet/files/FactsheetDisplay.asp?ID=18 .

[57] Animal Abuse and Violent Offending, at http://www.ncjrs.gov/html/ojjdp/jjbul2001_9_2/intro.html .

[58]   Criminologists Find Link Between Animal Cruelty, Later Violence, at http://www.animalsvoice.com/PAGES/writes/intros/link_between.html

[59] Randour, What We Know About the Link Between Animal Abuse and Human Violence, at http://www.animalsvoice.com/PAGES/writes/editorial/features/link/randour_link.html .

[60] Animal Abuse and Human Abuse: Partners in Crime, at http://www.helpinganimals.com/Factsheet/files/FactsheetDisplay.asp?ID=18 .

[61] Randour, What We Know About the Link Between Animal Abuse and Human Violence, at http://www.animalsvoice.com/PAGES/writes/editorial/features/link/randour_link.html .

[62]   Id .

[63] Animal Cruelty/Human Violence: The Link, at http://www.peteducation.com/article.cfm?cls=0&cat=1495&articleid=3120 .

[64] Animal abuse predictor of domestic violence, at http://www.chronicleforums.com/Forum/showthread.php?p=2448275#post2448275 .

[65] Canary in a Coal Mine: The Connection Between Animal Abuse and Human Violence, at http://www.vet.upenn.edu/schoolresources/communications/publications/bellwether/58/connection.html .

[66] Understanding the Link® between violence to people and animals , at http://www.americanhumane.org/site/PageServer?pagename=nr_fact_sheets_link .

[67] Animal Abuse and Human Abuse: Partners in Crime, at http://www.helpinganimals.com/Factsheet/files/FactsheetDisplay.asp?ID=18 .

[68] Animal Cruelty and Family Violence, at http://www.helpinganimals.com/ga_abuseFamily.asp .

[69] Id .

[70] Animal Abuse and Human Abuse: Partners in Crime, at http://www.helpinganimals.com/Factsheet/files/FactsheetDisplay.asp?ID=18 .

[71] Id .

[72] Id .

[73] Id .

[74] Id .

[75] Id .

[76] Canary in a Coal Mine: The Connection Between Animal Abuse and Human Violenc, at http://www.vet.upenn.edu/schoolresources/communications/publications/bellwether/58/connection.html .

[77] Id.

[78] Robyn Watts, Esq ., Domestic Violence and Animal Abuse , ASPCA, at http://www.aspca.org/site/PageServer?pagename=edu_resources_domestic (last visited June 27, 2007).

[79] Animal Abuse and Violent Offending, at http://www.ncjrs.gov/html/ojjdp/jjbul2001_9_2/page6.html .

[80] The Animal Abuse-Human Violence Link, at http://www.paws.org/help/report/connection.php .

[81] Animal Cruelty and Family Violence: Making the Connection, at http://www.hsus.org/hsus_field/first_strike_the_connection_between_animal_cruelty_and_human_violence/elder_abuse_and_animal_cruelty/ .

[82] Id.

[83] Id.[84] Animal Cruelty, Human Violence Linked in Humane Society Study, U.S. Department of Health and Human Services, Administration for Children & Families, at http://cbexpress.acf.hhs.gov/articles.cfm?article_id=316&issue_id=2001-07 (last viewed June 27, 2007).

[85] Id .

[86] Id .

[87] Animal Cruelty and Family Violence: Making the Connection, at http://www. hsus.org/hsus_field/first_strike_the_connection_between_animal_cruelty_and_human_ violence/elder_abuse_and_animal_cruelty/ .

[88] Animal Cruelty/Domestic Violence Fact Sheet , The Humane Society of the United States, at http://www.hsus.org/hsus_field/first_strike_the_connection_between_ animal_cruelty_and_human_violence/animal_cruelty_and_family_violence_making_ the_connection/animal_crueltydomestic_violence_fact_sheet.html (last viewed June 27, 2007).

[89] Id .

[90] Id .

[91] Id .

[92] Id .

[93] Id .

[94] Id .

[95] Id .

[96] Id .

[97] Frank R. Ascione, Ph.D, et al, The Abuse of Animals and Domestic Violence: A National Survey of Shelters for Women Who Are Battered , Utah State University, at http://www.vachss.com/guest_dispatches/ascione_1.html (last visited June 27, 2007).

[98] Animal Cruelty and Family Violence: Making the Connection , The Humane Society of the United States, at http://www.hsus.org/hsus_field/first_strike_the_ connection_between_animal_cruelty_and_human_violence/animal_cruelty_and_ family_violence_making_the_connection/ (last viewed on June 27, 2007).

[99] Animal Cruelty and Family Violence, at http://www.helpinganimals.com/ ga_abuseFamily.asp .

[100] Animal Abuse and Violent Offending, at http://www.ncjrs.gov/html/ojjdp/ jjbul2001_9_2/page6.html .

[101] Animal Cruelty and Family Violence, at http://www.helpinganimals.com/ ga_abuseFamily.asp .

[102] Children and Animal Cruelty: What Parents Should Know, at http://www. hsus.org/hsus_field/first_strike_the_connection_between_animal_cruelty_and_human_ violence/children_and_animal_cruelty_what_parents_should_know.html .

[103] Animal Abuse and Violent Offending, at http://www.ncjrs.gov/html/ojjdp/ jjbul2001_9_2/page7.html .

[104] Id. at http://www.ncjrs.gov/html/ojjdp/jjbul2001_9_2/page6.html .

[105] Animal Cruelty and Family Violence, at http://www.helpinganimals.com/ ga_abuseFamily.asp .

[106] Id.

[107] Animal Cruelty and Family Violence: Making the Connection, at http://www. hsus.org/hsus_field/first_strike_the_connection_between_animal_cruelty_and_human_ violence/animal_cruelty_and_family_violence_making_the_connection/ .

[108] The Animal Abuse-Human Violence Link, at http://www.paws.org/help/ report/connection.php .

[109] Animal Cruelty/Human Violence: The Link, at http://www.peteducation.com/ article.cfm?cls=0&cat=1495&articleid=3120 .

[110] Animal Abuse and Violent Offending, at http://www.ncjrs.gov/html/ojjdp/ jjbul2001_9_2/page7.html .

[111] Animal Cruelty and Family Violence: Making the Connection , The Humane Society of the United States, at http://www.hsus.org/hsus_field/first_strike_the_ connection_between_animal_cruelty_and_human_violence/animal_cruelty_and_ family_violence_making_the_connection/ .

[112] Animal Abuse and Violent Offending, at http://www.ncjrs.gov/html/ojjdp/ jjbul2001_9_2/page7.html .

[113] Canary in a Coal Mine: The Connection Between Animal Abuse and Human Violence, at http://www.vet.upenn.edu/schoolresources/communications/publications/ bellwether/58/connection.html .

[114] Animal Abuse and Human Abuse: Partners in Crime , People for the Ethical Treatment of Animals, at http://www.helpinganimals.com/factsheet/files/ FactsheetDisplay.asp?ID=132 (last viewed June 27, 2007).

[115] Weizel, Animal abuse predictor of domestic violence , at http://www. chronicleforums.com/Forum/showthread.php?p=2448275#post2448275 .

[116] Animal Abuse and Human Abuse: Partners in Crime, at http://www. helpinganimals.com/factsheet/files/FactsheetDisplay.asp?ID=132 .

[117] Canary in a Coal Mine: The Connection Between Animal Abuse and Human Violence, at http://www.vet.upenn.edu/schoolresources/communications/publications/ bellwether/58/connection.html .

[118] Cruelty to animals may lead to child abuse, at http://khastv.com/modules/ news/article.php?storyid=9304 .

[119] Id.

[120] Animal Abuse and Human Abuse: Partners in Crime, at http://www. helpinganimals.com/factsheet/files/FactsheetDisplay.asp?ID=132 .

[121] Animal Abuse and Violent Offending , at http://www.ncjrs.gov/html/ojjdp/ jjbul2001_9_2/page9.html .

5

Eating Meat Is Animal Abuse

The video lasts all of 12 seconds: A stray cat — after being lured by a young man's outstretched hand — is suddenly and violently kicked, its body propelled through the air, clearing a small fence and landing about 20 feet away, to a chorus of cackling laughter.

The man, Andre Robinson, was soon arrested.

Had it been a person he kicked, Mr. Robinson, 22, most likely would have received a quick plea bargain requiring no jail time — if, that is, he had even been arrested.

SELECTIVE COMPASSION

BECAUSE IT IS EASIER TO CONDEMN CITIZENS IN OTHER NATIONS FOR CONSUMING DOGS, AFTER YOU'VE JUST HAD A HAM SANDWICH FOR LUNCH

But now, every time Mr. Robinson has appeared in court in Brooklyn, animal-rights activists have surrounded him, attending his hearings and calling for a jail sentence. He has not even received a plea offer from prosecutors, which is extremely rare in misdemeanor cases.

Mr. Robinson, who has pleaded not guilty to a misdemeanor animal cruelty charge, has admitted to the police that he kicked the cat at the Brevoort Houses in Bedford-Stuyvesant, Brooklyn, where he lives, and then posted a video of the kick on Facebook. He has not explained why he kicked the cat.

The reaction to what the accused cat kicker did is understandable and laudable. It is nothing short of terrible that anyone would harm a defenseless animal. After all, we all believe that it is morally wrong to inflict unnecessary suffering on animals. Although we may disagree about when it is necessary to impose suffering and death on animals, we all agree that whatever pleasure Robinson got from kicking the cat cannot constitute necessity.

Or do we?

We kill and eat more than 58 billion animals a year worldwide, not counting fish. We don't need to eat animals. No one maintains that it is necessary for optimal human health. The conservative Academy of Nutrition and Dietetics acknowledges that "appropriately planned vegetarian diets, including total vegetarian or vegan diets, are healthful, nutritionally adequate and may provide health benefits in the prevention and treatment of certain diseases." The American Heart Association and Mayo Clinic agree.

And the animals we consume as food—including those used to make the supposedly more "humane" products sold at upscale supermarkets—are subjected to terrible suffering and horrible deaths. Indeed, the animals we use for food suffer just as much — if not more — than King, whom Robinson so callously kicked.

The only justification that we have for that suffering is palate pleasure. We enjoy the taste of animal foods; we find them convenient. There is no necessity for this suffering and death.

So how are we any different from Andre Robinson?

We aren't.

There is no morally coherent difference between the cat who was kicked and the chicken, pig, cow or fish that most people will eat today.

The FBI has announced that it will track "animal abuse" as a separate crime, the New York City Police Department has taken over responsibility for "animal abuse" complaints, and the Brooklyn DA is using the case to make a statement to "folks who think that they can just abuse any type of animal."

This is all laudable but it is nonsensical. We are a society that abuses billions of animals for no good reason whatsoever. We excuse ourselves by pretending that people like Robinson are "abusers" and the rest of us are really "humane" and care about animals.

Robinson will be prosecuted for violating a statute that prohibits "unjustifiably" harming animals. What he is accused of doing was not justifiable. The problem is what the rest of us do is not any more justifiable.

Remember football player Michael Vick? People hate him to this day for engaging in dog fighting. Or how about Kisha Curtis, who gained international condemnation for throwing her emaciated dog, Patrick, down a trash chute in Newark? Patrick is still used as a symbol by those who claim that we must pursue "animal abuse" more aggressively. All of these cases have resulted in an overwhelming online response, just as stories about the eating of dogs and cats in China or Korea, or the killing of dolphins in Japan, result in comments that "those people" are barbaric — made by people who have no problem exploiting pigs, cows, chicken and fish.

The Robinson case presents an opportunity for us to examine our fundamental views about animal ethics. Otherwise, this is just about fetishizing dogs and cats, or demonizing those whom we arbitrarily designate as "barbaric."

Source

Gary L. Francione: The Abolitionist Approach to Animal Rights, October 2, 2014

Stephanie Cliffordsept, He Kicked A Stray Cat, And Activists Growled, Newyork Times, September 29, 2014

Daily Mail Reporter, 6 May 2014

6

Meat Is Murder

Meat Eaters Have Blood On Their Hands

You Are A Party To The Crime Even If You Personally Do Not Do It

M eat is murder as it can only be obtained by killing a sentient being, unless of course you eat a carrion. And killing can never be humane. Just as there can be no such thing as honest stealing or kind-hearted rape.

And meat production, especially in the modern age, can hardly be called a benevolent activity. It is industrialization of cruelty and institutionalization of barbarism. Cruelty has always existed in human society but in the modern age it has taken the shape of a global industry. People always killed animals for food, entertainment and fur but killing in mechanized industrial slaughterhouses is a modern invention. Animals were never transported thousands of miles and neither existed global marketing networks in animal products.

END THE SLAUGHTER

Billions of animals are raised in appalling conditions that would have people thrown in jail if performed on dogs or cats, but farm animals are specifically excluded from Animal Welfare Acts. There's far too much information regarding animal treatment to give an accurate picture in just a few pages but meat production, like any other industry, is one that is driven purely by profit. It exhibits complete disregard for animals' feelings and the environment.

Animal transport is particularly cruel. Animals may be transported several times during their lifetimes, and they may travel hundreds or even thousands of miles during a single trip. Long journeys are very stressful and contribute to diseases and even death. A distinct disease called "Shipping fever" is common and costs livestock producers billion every year. Many get crushed or freeze to death in winter or die of dehydration in summer.

After a long journey, without food or water, those still alive arrive at the slaughterhouse which examplifies hell on earth. Modern mechanized slaughterhouses kill thousands of animals every hour. The high speed of the assembly line makes it increasingly difficult to treat animals with any semblance of humaneness. A Meat & Poultry article states, "Good handling is extremely difficult if equipment is 'maxed out' all the time. It is impossible to have a good attitude toward animals if employees have to constantly overexert themselves, and thus transfer all that stress right down to the animals, just to keep up with the line."

Prior to being hung up by their back legs and bled to death, animals are supposed to be rendered unconscious. One common

The effects of meat proteins can undoubtedly be seen in aggression, violence, hatred and moral insensitivity. The vegetarian, on the other hand, builds the foundations for an attitude of tolerance, gentleness, sociability and a spirit of sharing. Experts speaking out against the use of meat proteins can now call on support from the chemistry of neurotransmitters and from neurobiology, two scientific disciplines that explain how such foods cause certain human behaviours. Among other things, we should reject the idea that violence is innate in humans: no-one is born aggressive or evil, but we can become so by eating meat.

~ Armando D'Elia, President, AVI Scientific Committee

practice is 'stunning' which is usually done by a mechanical blow to the head. However, the procedure is terribly imprecise, and inadequate stunning is inevitable. As a result, conscious animals are often hung upside down, kicking and struggling, while a slaughterhouse worker makes another attempt to render them unconscious.

This is detailed in an April 2001 Washington Post article, which describes typical slaughter plant conditions:

> The cattle were supposed to be dead before they got to Moreno. But too often they weren't.
>
> They blink. They make noises, he said softly. The head moves, the eyes are wide and looking around. Still Moreno would cut. On bad days, he says, dozens of animals reached his station clearly alive and conscious. Some would survive as far as the tail cutter, the belly ripper, the hide puller. They die, said Moreno, piece by piece...
>
> "In plants all over the United States, this happens on a daily basis," said Lester Friedlander, a veterinarian and formerly chief government inspector at a Pennsylvania hamburger plant. "I've seen it happen. And I've talked to other veterinarians. They feel it's out of control."

This is the fate of over 60 billion animals that are slaughtered for human consumption every year.

In factory farms, millions of animals and birds are confined and tortured in hellish conditions, are deprived of sunlight, fresh air and natural food and the freedom to walk or fly. Thus we create an environment for the spread of virus and disease. And at the whiff of an infection, statutorily kill millions of them in the name of 'culling'.

Millions of cows and pigs who make it to the slaughterhouse alive are unable to walk off the trucks. Called "downers," a former slaughterhouse worker describes the customary welcome for these animals:

"... they beat him with pipes, kick them, hit them with pieces of wood, stick them with knives. If he still won't move, you wrap the cable around his neck and drag them in with the hoist. You drag them while they're still alive." "And they stab cows in the butt to make 'em move. Break their tails. They beat them so bad. I've drug cows till their bones start breaking, while they were still alive. Bringing them around the corner and they get stuck up in the doorway, just pull them till their hide be ripped, till the blood just drip on the steel and concrete. Breaking their legs pulling them in. And the cow be crying with its tongue stuck out. They pull him till his neck just pop."

Source

Slaughterhouse: The Shocking Story of Greed, Neglect, And Inhumane Treatment Inside the U.S. Meat Industry, Gail A. Eisnitz

Grandin, T. and Deesing, M. "Humane Livestock Handling" 2008. Storey Publishing, North Adams, MA, USA.

Grandin, Temple (July 2010). "Improving the Movement of Cattle, Pigs, and Sheep during handling on farms, ranches, and slaughter plants"

Eisnitz, Gail A. Slaughterhouse. Prometheus Books, 1997, cited in Torres, Bob. Making a Killing. AK Press, 2007

7

'Meat-Eaters Are Terrorists'

- Chrissie Hynde

Rocker Chrissie Hynde has hit out at meat-eaters, branding them the true "terrorists" of this world. Speaking at a London gala organised by animal rights group PETA (People for the Ethical Treatment of Animals) in June 2006, the Pretenders frontwoman delivered an impassioned speech to a star-studded crowd including fellow campaigners Gillian Anderson, Sadie Frost and Pamela Anderson. The 54-year-old even declared she is prepared to be imprisoned for her beliefs. She said, "We know that all meat-eaters are terrorists and PETA declared its war on terror years and years ago. I'd rather go to jail with them than go out clubbing with any person I know." Hynde was presented with an award for her ceaseless efforts to improve fast food giant Kentucky Fried Chicken's treatment of animals.

Slaughterhouse Operations - Legalized Terrorism

Barely a few years into it, the twenty-first century is already clearly marked as the "Age of Terrorism." The attacks of September 11, 2001 marked a salient turning point in the history of the U.S. and indeed of global geopolitics. The U.S. declared its number one priority to be the "War on Terrorism," and its domestic, national, and international policies have changed accordingly. In his address to the nation shortly after the 9/11 attacks, Bush used the terms "terror," "terrorism," and "terrorist" thirty-two times without ever defining what he meant.

In the amorphous name of "terrorism," wars are being fought, geopolitical dynamics are shifting, the U.S. is aggressively reasserting its traditional imperialist role as it defies international law and world bodies, and the state is sacrificing liberties to "security."

One of the most commonly used words in the current vocabulary, "terrorism" is also one of the most abused terms. Steve Best defines terrorism "as any intentional act to injure or kill a living, sentient, innocent being for scientific, political or economic purposes." This is a sane, sensible and rational definition. Going by this definition, there are a lot more terrorists in the world than those on FBI's list. Practically every one fits as a terrorist in this definition.

Animals which are captured, enslaved, tortured and slaughtered are being "terrorized". Indeed animals are sentient - when they scream in labs, when they suffer in rodeos and when they stand before the butcher... they are all in terror of our brutal power over them.

In this way, not all terrorists fight with guns and bombs, and not all terrorists fight strictly for political gain. There are men and women in this world who are terrorists in another real sense.

Virtually all definitions of terrorism, even by "progressive" human rights champions, outright banish from consideration the most excessive violence of all—that which the human species unleashes against all nonhuman species. Speciesism is so ingrained and entrenched in the human mind that the human mass murder of animals does not even appear on the conceptual radar screen. Any attempt to perceive nonhuman animals as innocent victims of violence and human animals as terrorists is rejected with derision.

Nations As Terrorist States

But if terrorism is linked to intentional violence inflicted on innocent persons for ideological, political, or economic motivations, and nonhuman animals also are "persons"—subjects of a life—then the human war against animals is terrorism. Every individual who terrifies, injures, tortures, and/or kills an animal is a terrorist; fur farms, factory farms, foie gras, vivisection, and other exploitative operations are terrorist industries; and governments that support these industries are terrorist states. The true weapons of mass

destruction are the gases, rifles, stun guns, cutting blades, and forks and knives used to experiment on, kill, dismember, and consume animal bodies.

The anti-terror crusader, US alone kills over one million animals per hour who are cruelly raised, handled, transported, stocked and killed.

Each year in USA alone,

• Over 10 billion farmed animals are killed for food consumption (which translates to over 1 million animals per hour);

• 17–70 million animals are killed for testing and experimentation;

• Over 100 million are killed for hunting; and

• 7–8 million animals are trapped or raised in confinement for their fur.

Mahatma Gandhi rightly puts it, "the greatness of a nation is judged by the way it treats its animals".

This crime against creation can never go unpunished. Ordinary laws can be circumvented or courts can be bribed but no one can

We only need to look as far as the slaughterhouse workers themselves to see the oxymoron of the term 'humane slaughter'. A slaughterhouse worker quoted in the book 'Slaughterhouse' states:

"Pigs on the kill floor have come up and nuzzled me like a puppy. Two minutes later I had to kill them – beat them to death with a pipe."

Rare vision, from a British documentary, The Task of Blood, contained interviews with the people tasked with taking the lives of these animals. One of these men stated:

"I kill animals for a living, all day, every day, and I really like my job. You can get away with murder every day and not get arrested for it. Some people think I'm sick [doing] what I do. But they don't think I'm sick when it's on their plate."

Later he is seen holding a knife towards the neck of a sheep. He turns and smiles to the camera. "This is the fun part," he says as he slashes the knife across the sheep's throat.

escape the stringent laws of material nature. Unnecessary killing of even an ant is a serious crime.

Reference

Femalefirst.co.uk, 2 July 2006, © 2014 First Active Media Ltd.

Thalif Deen. "Politics: U.N. Member States Struggle to Define Terrorism", Inter Press Service, 25 July 2005.

Spring Fever: The Illusion of Islamic Democracy, Andrew C. McCarthy - 2013

Hoffman, Bruce (1998). Inside Terrorism. Columbia University Press.

Disorders and Terrorism, National Advisory Committee on Criminal Justice Standards and Goals (Washington D.C.:1976)

8

You Are Literally What You Eat

Slaughterhouse Products Are Imbued With Cruelty

Eating meat may lead to behavior changes. According to Dr. John Briffa, a medical doctor who leans toward a holistic approach to healthcare, mood and behavior are directly related to the food we eat. People who rely on sugar and high-fat foods such as meat are more prone to violence and depression. The nutrients found in fruits, vegetables and whole grains are vital to maintaining a healthy emotional balance. Mood swings are more easily controlled as well when you eat a balanced diet of fat, protein and carbohydrates.

Some proponents of vegetarian diets say that eating meat is an aberrant behavior for humans because our bodies are not made to process meat. The act of tearing apart a piece of meat for consumption in and of itself leads to aggressive behavior. At the same time, the physical byproducts of a meat-eating diet, including increased cholesterol levels, may lead to varying degrees of behavior changes.

Aggression

According to physician and nutrition specialist John McDougall, eating meat is a masculine behavior, with its butchering and killing most often associated with aggressive male behavior. Taking control over a living thing bestows a level of brute power in humans and can lead to more aggressive behavior when the meat is consumed. Eating a large steak dripping with blood can stir feelings of virility in men as well as strength, passion and aggressive actions.

Meat - An Ayurvedic Perspective

Ayurveda considers diet as an important aspect of life which is in its own right capable of promoting or disturbing balance in the physiology.

The ancient textual authorities make many references to the kinds of meat that may be appropriate for balancing a myriad of imbalances.

The question arises: "Is it still okay to eat flesh?" Ayurveda holds that digestion is the process at the root of all health. Heavy foods are harder to digest than lighter foods. Our goal is to make digestion easy and to get more energy from food than it requires to digest it. The heaviness of flesh tends to dull digestion and mental alertness (called tamasic).

Modern pathophysiology has an explanation for this effect. When digestion is weak there tends to be a development and proliferation of anaerobic bacteria. The presence of the bacteria promotes the conversion of meat proteins into harmful substances, such as phenol and "pseudo monoamines" such as octopamine (many normal neurotransmitters are monoamines; e.g. dopamine. These "pseudo monoamines" compete with monoamines for receptor sites in the brain. By occupying a receptor site the cell is prompted to perform some action, which depends upon the specific nature of the occupying molecules. Because "pseudo monoamines" do not act as monoamines, by passing on impulses in a nerve, the impulse is effectively deactivated (not sent on to the next nerve receptor--axon).

This process leads to the brain "shutting down" and is experienced as dullness by those eating meats and having poor digestion.

Meats and eggs also have a quality that tends to promote aggressive and angry behavior (called rajasic). Some of this influence comes from the natural presence of arachidonic acid (an inflammatory substance), and also from steroids and other substances injected into or fed cattle, etc. Animals are the end point of the food chain for many kinds of poisons in the environment--including, pesticides, herbicides, etc. The conditions of slaughter of an animal

A TORMENTED SLAVE TO THE DAIRY INDUSTRY FOR HER ENTIRE SHORT LIFE, SHE HAS GIVEN ALL THE MILK THAT HER BODY COULD GENERATE

release stress hormones in the animal, which affects us. We express the qualities of the foods we ingest. We are what we eat in very literal way. Balance in the physiology means evenness and alertness (called sattvic). Meats do not promote evenness, alertness, etc. Meats tax the digestive process by their heaviness, promote aggressiveness, inflammatory changes, and tend to impede elimination (leading to putrefaction).

Modern research findings have uncovered some disturbing correlations: Higher incidence of stomach cancer has been associated with predominantly fish eating cultures. Multiple

"After they left me, the hogs would go up a ramp to a tank where they're dunked in 140° water. By the time they hit the scalding tank, they're still fully conscious." They get up to the scalding tank, hit the water, & start kicking & screaming. A rotating pushes them under. I am not sure if they burn to death before they drown, but it takes them a couple of minutes to stop thrashing." Here's your bacon - and your victims.
~ Tommy Vladak, slaughter plant worker,

Sclerosis symptoms have been linked to dietary intake of animal fats. Incidence of colon cancer is higher among meat eating cultures than among non-meat eating cultures. It is believed that meats in the process of metabolism foster viri proliferation.

There is evidence that the presence of butyrate is inversely related to the incidence of colon cancer. Healthy bacteria in the colon digest vegetable matter fiber and convert it into butyrate (butyric acid). Hence, if you don't eat vegetables, butyrate will not be formed and cancer risk rises. In addition, problems

> "YOU CALL IT PORK, I CALL IT PIG.
> YOU CALL IT BEEF, I CALL IT COW.
> YOU CALL IT VEAL, I CALL IT BABY.
> YOU CALL IT LEATHER, I CALL IT SKIN.
> YOU CALL IT FOOD, I CALL IT MURDER.
> YOU CALL IT FASHION, I CALL IT STEALING.
> YOU CALL YOURSELF A HUMAN,
> I CALL YOU A BARBARIAN".

with cholesterol, obesity, heart disease etc., seem to be significantly lower for those eating a vegetarian diet.

The China Study, by Colin Campbell, documents these risks and implicates all animal proteins, generically. We do not introduce these data to scare people away from eating flesh, rather we just want

> *The propaganda from the animal abusers is enormous. I mean when was the last time you turned on a TV and saw a commercial for shitake mushrooms? People singing and dancing down the streets having a good time eating mushrooms. How about alfalfa sprouts? Quinoa? (it's a seed) Radishes? Raspberries? Tofu? You don't see that stuff advertized on TV. What do you see instead? Have some more meat. Have some more cheese. Have some more meat on your cheese, double cheese, extra cheese and how about a little more cheese with your meat. Have some more cow's milk. Have some more eggs. And what do you see interspersed between those advertizements? Not feeling so well? Need to see a cancer specialist? How about a heart doctor? Need some Lipotor? Zocor? Crestor? Plavix? Need some diet pills? How about some energy drinks? Some Kaopectate? Tums? Pepto-Bismal? You've been duped. They're killing you, they're killing the animals and they're killing this planet...*
> *~Gary Yourofsky*

to introduce the idea that health is related to the food we eat. We feel livelier and more alert by eating foods rich in these qualities-- digestion produces more usable energy for activity from vegetarian foods. And that translates into a healthy body and mind, resulting in the actions in the mode of goodness.

Reference

Michael S. Dick © 1994 Ayurveda-florida.

Linda Ray, Livestrong.com, May 26, 2011

Jeff Collins, Diet And Psyche, November 1999, Michigan Monitor

9

"Can't Wait For Feeling You Get When U Just Killed Some1"

Tweet of A Generation Brought Up On Slaughterhouse Products

Thousands of teenagers from all over the world are rushing to the killing fields of Syria and Iraq, to experience the thrill of killing and torture. In the name of waging a holy war, they are also killing each other. This is reflective of a lost generation, addicted to violence and abuse.

British citizens and other jihadists fighting in Syria have been involved in the beating and execution of fellow rebels.

It comes after a man from London has posted a torture video on Facebook, which appears to show the beating of prisoners.

The man - believed to be with a jihadist rebel group and originally from West London - has uploaded a video in which he claimed to have tortured a fighter with the Free Syrian Army - which is backed by the west.

Alongside images of the fighter tied to a car tyre and being hit with an iron bar, the 'jihadist' writes that he launched the attack after he 'insulted his brothers'

The prisoner is heard protesting his innocence as he is apparently beaten across the legs with an metal bar, and is stamped on

He said: 'Some FSA are starting to feel they run things! This FSA scum never thought we wud jump out at them and pick them up after saying some abusive words to our brothers.'

'Two then got ahead of themselves and swore at Allah, at this point there was no stopping us LOL [laugh out loud] although we where told to just leave them.'

He shouts that he is not a 'kuffar', a non-believer, and that he is a 'mujahid' - a Muslim fighter - and begs them not to kill him.

Got these criminals today. Insha'Allah will be killed tomorow. Cant wait for that feeling when U just killed some1

In a separate picture posted on Twitter by another British citizen in Syria, three prisoners are seen blindfolded, alongside the words: 'Got these criminals today. Insha'Allah [God willing] they will be killed tomorrow. Can't wait for that feeling when u just killed some1'

The same user then posted a picture of a blood soaked hand along with the words: 'My first time!'

Spending As Much Time Killing Each Other As They Do The Enemy

An ISIS deserter has claimed he fled the terrorist organisation because he was appalled at the level of violence and their willingness to kill innocent women and children.

Abu Almouthanna, 27, escaped from Syria across the border to Turkey where he is under the constant threat of death.

The Syrian national said he had spent three years fighting against the Basher al-Assad regime when he was eventually forced to join ISIS.

He said after joining ISIS he was paid $150 a month in wages but was forced to adhere to strict rules, the breaching of which would lead to a death sentence.

He told Fox News that he had no problem in killing Christians, Kurds and Yazidis, but he had issues with attacking rival jihadis and their families.

It was during this period that Almouthanna met some of the thousands of radicalized Western fighters who have flocked to Syria and Iraq to join Islamic State, he said. Three Frenchmen and a Briton who he bunked with were given regular Arabic lessons and studied the Koran endlessly. But it was their sheer bloodlust that set them apart, he said.

"From Day One, they joked about cutting heads and making the enemy pay," Almouthanna said.

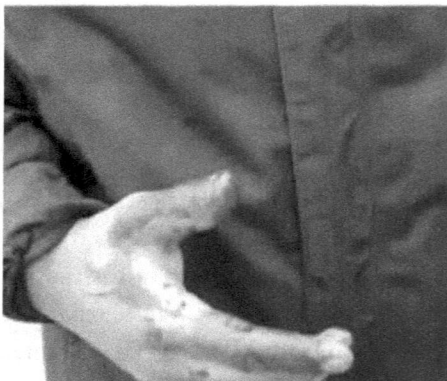

My first time!

To spread terror among the civilian populations of small villages, Islamic State fighters would conduct public beheadings, he said. Townspeople would crowd into the main square to watch, bringing their children along, he said. Islamic State members would fight over who would wield the blade.

The butchery of battle gave way to "special" camaraderie when the fighting ended. Islamic State fighters would recount their exploits, the nameless innocent victims they'd killed and joke about women.

In Raqqa, Islamic State prisons were packed with captives being tortured with cattle prods, beaten with sticks and burned to death.

After one battle, Almouthanna recalled, Islamic State forces took 300 prisoners, including women and children. They held them for a day, before deeming them a burden and mowing them down in the desert, he said.

Almouthanna told Fox News that he made his decision to leave following the five-week battle for Markada.

He said: 'By the end, we were killing everything and everyone, including women and children in surrounding villages or left in the town. The fighters killed civilians with merciless glee, and didn't have to be ordered to do so. Those who try to leave are easily replaced by foreign fighters pouring in daily.'

Schoolgirls Aged 14-16 Leave France, UK, Germany for Syria's Killing Fields

Hundreds of young women and girls are leaving their homes in western countries to join Islamic fighters in the Middle East, causing increasing concern among counter-terrorism investigators.

The Guardian has a fascinating report on Schoolgirl leaving their comfortable home to join the horrors of Syrian civil war.

Girls as young as 14 or 15 are travelling mainly to Syria to marry jihadis, bear their children and join communities of fighters, with a significant number taking up arms. Many are recruited via social media.

Women and girls appear to make up about 10% of those leaving Europe, North America and Australia to link up with jihadi groups, including Islamic State (Isis). France has the highest number of female jihadi recruits.

At least 40 women have left Germany to join Isis in Syria and Iraq in what appears to be a growing trend of teenagers becoming radicalised and travelling to the Middle East without their parents' permission. "The youngest was 13-years-old," Hans-Georg Maassen, president of the Federal Office for the Protection of the Constitution, told the Rheinische Post.

Karim Pakzad, of the French Institute of International and Strategic Relations, said some young women had "an almost romantic idea of war and warriors.

"There's a certain fascination even with the head and throat-cutting. It's an adventure."

Some British women and girls have posted pictures of themselves carrying AK-47s, grenades and in one case a severed head, as they pledge allegiance to ISIS. But they are also tweeting pictures of food, restaurants and sunsets to present a positive picture of the life awaiting young women in an attempt to lure more from the UK.

Women already living amid Isis fighters used social media adeptly to portray Syria as a utopia and to attract foreign women to join their "sisterhood in the caliphate", she said.

But the reality was very different, she said. Both Bloom and Rolf Tophoven, director of Germany's Institute for Terrorism Research and Security Policy, said reports indicated that women had been raped, abused, sold into slavery or forced to marry. Many family members are trying their best to get their kids back, with some even travelling to the war zone.

Reference

Daily Mail Reporter, 11 February 2014

Darren Boyle For Dailymail, 7 November 2014

Benjamin HallNovember 06, 2014, FoxNews

Mike "Mish" Shedlock, Global Economic Analysis

Harriet Sherwood, Sandra Laville, Kim Willsher in Paris, Ben Knight in Berlin, Maddy French in Vienna and Lauren Gambino in New York, The Guardian, Monday 29 September 2014

10

Source Of Fascination

With The Head And Throat-Cutting

TV presenter Susannah Constantine shared a picture of ten-year-old daughter Cece proudly clutching a dead duck and with her face smeared with blood to mark her first kill. The little girl is also shown holding guns and taking part in hunts in a series of photos dating back almost a year and published on her and her mother's public Instagram profiles. The photographs are accompanied by captions such as 'First duck' and 'No food left after Christmas. Cece off to save the day'.

Miss Constantine has been condemned by animal rights campaigners, who claimed the pictures call into question her abilities as a mother and branded the decision to let a child hunt 'depressing', 'irresponsible' and 'dangerous'.

The 52-year-old's privileged background and lifelong passion for hunting has done little to appease her critics, with a spokesman for Animal Aid saying there is 'no justification for putting a weapon into the hands of a child'.

The sentiment was echoed by a spokesman for People for the Ethical Treatment of Animals, who said: 'Susannah's mothering skills have to be called into question, as she's evidently failed to convey the most basic lesson of "Do unto others as you would have them do unto you".'

Michael Stephenson, of the League Against Cruel Sports, added: 'We believe parents have a responsibility to teach their kids to respect and enjoy wildlife. We don't believe children should be killing wildlife full stop and have always expressed concern at children being exposed to blood sports.'

Miss Constantine has long been vocal about her love of hunting. In an interview as far back as 1990, she said: '... it is relaxing because when you're in the saddle you have to concentrate entirely on what you are doing'.

Source
Sam Creighton For The Daily Mail, 9 November 2014.
London Evening Standard, 08 December 2014

I want to ask you to use some empathy right now. When I say empathy what I'm saying is place yourself in the position of the animals and start to view this issue from the animal's point of view - from the victim's point of view. When you examine any form of injustice, whether humans are victims or animals are victims, please remember the victim's point of view...
~Gary Yourofsky

11

Use Of Child Soldiers In Conflicts

Rising Significantly

A report released by the United Nations in July documented more than 4,000 cases of children being recruited and used in conflicts last year - but said thousands more are estimated to have been forced to join armies and rebel groups around the globe.

Secretary-General Ban Ki-moon's annual report on children and armed conflict adds Nigeria's notorious extremist group Boko Haram to the U.N. 'list of shame.'

It now includes eight government forces and 51 armed groups that recruit or use, kill or maim, commit sexual violence or rape against children in conflicts, or attack schools or hospitals.

The report said the recruitment and use of children in armed conflict remained prevalent in 2013 and those who commit grave violations against children, especially sexual violence, usually don't face justice.

Leila Zerrougui, the special representative for children and armed conflict, told a news conference launching the report that advances by Islamist extremists in Iraq 'are creating extremely volatile and dangerous conditions for children.'

She said the secretary-general has listed four new parties for recruiting and using children: Islamic State of Iraq and the Levant, al-Qaida affiliated Jahbat al-Nusra, the ultraconservative Islamic rebel group Ahrar al-Sham, and the Kurdish People Protection Units or YPG.

Reference

Daily Mail, John Hall, 8 December 2014

Child Soldiers: An Affront To Humanity, UN Report, 2014

State of the World's Children, UNICEF, 2013

12

Some More

Spine-chilling Statistics

The link between animal abuse and violence towards people is supported by studies,which have shown that:

• 100% of sexual homicide offenders examined had a history of cruelty towards animals.[1]

• 70% of all animal abusers have committed at least one other criminal offense and almost 40% have committed violent crimes against people.[2]

• 63.3% of men who had committed crimes of aggression admitted to cruelty to animals.[3]

• 48% of rapists and 30% of child molesters reported committing animal abuse during childhood or adolescence.[4]

• 36% of assaultive women reported cruelty to animals while 0% of non-assaultive women did.[5]

• 25% of violent, incarcerated men reported higher rates of "substantial cruelty to animals" in childhood than a comparison group of non-incarcerated men (0%).[6]

• Men who abused animals were five times more likely to have been arrested for violence towards humans, four times more likely to have committed property crimes, and three times more likely to have records for drug and disorderly conduct offenses.[7]

Reference

1 Animal Abuse and Human Abuse: Partners in Crime, at

http://www.helpinganimals.com/Factsheet/files/FactsheetDisplay.asp?ID=18.

2 The Animal Abuse-Human Violence Link, at http://www.paws.org/help/report/ connection.php.

3 Animal Abuse and Violent Offending, at http://www.ncjrs.gov/html/ojjdp/ jjbul2001_9_2/page4.html.

4 Id.

5 Id.

6 Id.

7 Randour, What We Know About the Link, Between Animal Abuse and Human Violence.

13

Slaughterhouse Workers

More Likely To Be Violent

Meatworkers are more prone to violence and women are the worst, according to a new study.

People who work in abattoirs are more likely to be desensitised to suffering, which in turn could make them more likely to be violent towards humans, the research published in the Society and Animals journal found.

Overseas research has found that towns with abattoirs have higher rates of domestic violence and violent crimes including murder and rape, which prompted the Australian team to investigate the situation.

Flinders University senior sociology lecturer Dr Nik Taylor said it had been established that the more positive a person's attitude to animals, the lower their aggression levels, and that the reverse is also true – if you're cruel to animals, you're more likely to be violent to humans.

She found that meatworkers' aggression levels were "so high they're similar to the scores... for incarcerated populations".

"They're a pretty angry bunch and that anger shows," she said, adding that one of their "jawdropping" findings was that women in the meatworking industry were even more aggressive than the men.

"We've got some very, very angry women. Maybe they need to prove themselves by being more macho," she said.

The study included meatworkers and farmers, and they found that while farmers had "utilitarian" attitudes towards animals they were less aggressive than the general community.

The authors used a "propensity for aggression" scale.

Dr Taylor said while their sample size was small – comprising 41 farmers and 26 meatworkers – it builds on existing research that has established a link between working in a slaughterhouse and being more aggressive and violence prone.

A 2010 study by Canadian criminologist Amy Fitzgerald found violent crimes including sexual assault and rape increase in towns once an abattoir moves in.

The University of Windsor professor compared statistics from

581 US counties to prove the link, and says labourers become desensitised to violence. She ruled out factors such as the influx of young men and immigrants, whom communities sometimes blamed.

Prof Fitzgerald said it wasn't the nature of repetitive and dangerous work, but the act of slaughtering an animal that was to blame for the increase in violence.

"The unique thing about (abattoirs) is that (workers are) not dealing with inanimate objects, but instead dealing with live animals coming in and then killing them, and processing what's left of them," she said.

Dr Taylor said the Australian findings showed more work needed to be done to assess the effect of working in abattoirs on both employees and the community.

Reference

News.com.au, January 23, 2013

Arluke, A., & Sanders, C. R. (1996). Regarding animals. Philadelphia: Temple University Press.

14

Killing For A Living

The Traumatic Consequences of Slaughterhouse Work

What is it like to work in a slaughterhouse? Most abattoirs use assembly lines to quickly and cheaply massacre and process the animals. Workers are paid very low wages, and the jobs are degrading, gruesome and repetitive. Employees must endure sickening scenes of blood, gore and death every day, and the working conditions are extremely dangerous.

Many slaughterhouse workers feel trapped in their jobs, having no other way to provide for their families. Such a traumatic occupation exacts a huge price – draining a worker's physical, emotional, mental and spiritual well-being. A person who worked in a chicken-processing plant in England describes his former job.

I did several kinds of jobs in the chicken factory. First my role was to hang the live chickens. They had to be put on a line that led to the slaughtering. If the job for this was already filled, then my task was to hang the already dead chickens.

The point is that, just like an animal, they made us work under very cold, very bad conditions. No break, no rest, no work clothes, nothing. I had to put on the only pair of rubber boots which had been taken off by the person before me. If they were wet from him, I just had to work also in wet rubber boots.

76

These obscene killing factories can be absolutely massive in size. The largest slaughterhouse in the world, operated by a company in the US, can butcher over 32,000 pigs a day. And in the US alone, 270 chickens are slain every second or about 8.5 billion chickens a year. To kill and process this many innocent beings, employees are under constant pressure to work quickly and keep the murderous assembly lines going.

Another person, a former employee recounts:

There were machines. There were machines everywhere.

These were very powerful machines that the person had to put the chicken inside one by one, from the right or left side. But your hands had to be fast there, like a machine. And even then, they were shouting a lot and were strict.

They were shouting at us, "Faster, faster!" If you weren't fast enough, you were told to leave.

But one aspect of abattoirs is even more revolting than the working conditions.

Because of the drastic sights in the factory, because of the torture of animals, the animals did not have a chance. And this was very disgusting and disturbing to us that every day just more, and more, and more of this.

We hanged the chickens every day, and I saw every day the large amount of meat, the carcasses, the bodies of that huge number, many thousands, many thousands of chickens. I reflected upon how many thousands of chicken go away in a month, in a year, and that all of these are living beings.

And to fulfill animal-torturing roles like this, this was a very bad sight. And it was very bad to think about the fact that we raise something only to be killed under such torturous conditions, and to eat it.

Witnessing countless deaths day after mind-numbing day is utterly devastating to one's mental state. In her report, "A

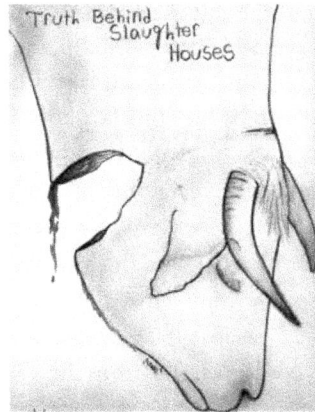

Slaughterhouse Nightmare: Psychological Harm Suffered by Slaughterhouse Employees and the Possibility of Redress through Legal Reform," Jennifer Dillard, a lawyer in the United States, examines some of the many psychological problems, including post-traumatic stress disorder, suffered by slaughterhouse workers.

And in her book, "Slaughterhouse," Gail A. Eisnitz, chief investigator for the Humane Farming Association, describes the crippling mental effects of this violent line of work. For many employees, the endless bloody murders they see at these factories of death continue to haunt them, even long after they leave their jobs.

We are sorry for what happened and that we also had to see this, what people do to an animal. We cannot forget what happened there and the things we did. It was a very bad experience for me.

And I do not wish this upon anyone. How they keep those animals, as we said, in the 21st century, and what they do to them, it's hideous. It is horrible. This is a horrible sight. It is like murder. Everything is covered in blood, and she (the chicken) is still alive. Her head is no longer there, but her body is still alive. And it's terrible.

Do the workers ever think about the feelings of the animals they slay? Former slaughterhouse employee Ed Calles, now a vegetarian, shares some of his personal experiences.

I grew up the son of a dock foreman in a beef slaughterhouse. When I got back home from the Vietnam War, I went to the slaughterhouse where my father was working, and took on some work. Back then I saw many things that were fairly disturbing, not knowing how de-sensitized I had become. I saw animals being led to their slaughter. That really impacted me.

Was this the purpose they were put on Earth for? I asked myself that question over and over as I saw them coming out of the cattle trucks and into the corrals and even jumping the corrals and fearing for their lives, running down the avenue, and taking on automobiles head-on, crashing into them. And this animal was in fear of her life. So, in seeing that, I was just aghast. How cruel! I mean, I had been back from the war and saw a lot of cruelty and death and killing and that sort of thing, and here I was, in need of a job, and I saw all this cruelty again.

Constantly surrounded by the animals' heart wrenching cries for help as well as blood, urine and feces, slaughterhouse employees often try to find ways to cope.

Eventually, I became desensitized. But in my heart of hearts, I knew there was something wrong here. I didn't know exactly what. Guys carried on in a bloodthirsty kind of lifestyle. During work, in the early morning hours, loading trucks with these animal carcasses, men drank all night long; (they were) severely intoxicated. But they did their job.

And I was offered a lot to drink, but I couldn't. Now looking back at it, I think they had to. Because it was their way of desensitizing themselves. I just wanted to be at peace with myself and everybody around me, but I just couldn't find it there.

In Ed Calles' experience, the brutal work often resulted in another outcome.

These men had episodes of rage and anger if little things didn't go their way. Many times there were drunken brawls over the smallest of things. And the toughest guy was the guy who picked up, the most amount of weight, that you just gave more respect to.

But a smaller little guy would pick up something and start swinging, I mean (swinging) hooks, (the) big hooks that these pieces of meat would roll down the dock to, for us to swing them, and cut them and load them. So many times there was an outbreak of a fight. And a lot of it just was not making much sense. And I had to find another way out, and eventually I did.

Slaughterhouse workers can become so unfeeling to death and devoid of compassion that they sometimes injure or kill animals simply for amusement. Les Ingram, a former slaughterhouse employee in the UK, recalls one such incident.

And so one young bloke I remember, he goes down in the lairage one day, and he's carrying a boning knife. And there are pens full of sheep. And he just stuck the knife through the bars and stabbed it into the side of a sheep. I said, "What did you do that for?"

When you're going into those places, killing animals is part of everyday life, because that's what happens there. So it must affect some people quite badly. Whether people manage to deal with it, and whatever the system they use to deal with it, some do (have it), but some don't.

Are people who live in the vicinity of a slaughterhouse also affected by the murderous atmosphere? Jaylene Musgrave, a vegan in Australia whose father worked in an abattoir, shares her childhood experience.

Each night, I'd go to sleep and you'd hear the cows mooing and you could just feel the fright and terror that they were going through. And I just felt sick all the time, knowing that these poor animals were being held captive and what they were going to go through. It just made me always anxious. And I never, ever want to live near anything like that, ever again.

While the employees in a slaughterhouse may be doing the killing, they are actually just one part of a system that supplies meat to consumers. Hence there's only one way we can end this murderous cycle: adopt a plant-based diet.

I actually think that anyone that consumes animal products should take time to visit an abattoir. The people that work in those situations are doing the dirty work for consumers. And I believe that if anyone who wants to eat meat had to slaughter their own animal, we'd have a lot more vegetarians in this world.

How do the workers handle their heinous jobs? What happens when an employee can't cope? Does working in an abattoir affect family life? Another former employee recalls:

If people have to kill a living, breathing, loving, gentle, innocent animal to put in their mouth, I think they will stop. Just that most people they don't know what cruel, gruesome thing in the slaughterhouse for the animals to be killed. They don't know it. It's out of their mind.

They don't even associate that piece of meat with the living, breathing, loving, gentle, kind, innocent, loving, living being. They don't associate. But if they have to go out and kill it for themselves, then I think they will stop.

Each year, 60 billion animals are murdered worldwide, most of them being killed by abattoir employees.

Such a traumatic occupation exacts a huge price – draining a worker's physical, emotional, mental and spiritual well-being.

According to US Department of Agriculture statistics, in 2008, 4,032 cows, 13,248 pigs and over one million chickens were killed every hour in the US. Hour after hour, day after day, slaughterhouse employees are engaged in this endless, bloody slaying of innocent animals.

Les Ingram, a former slaughterhouse worker in the UK, recalls the vicious process, which begins by stunning the animals with a bolt gun.

It's just like a tube that they just put on the head, and as it contacts, it explodes and pushes the bolt into the skull to make the hole where they put the pithing cane, which they push through the hole in the skull and then it curls up. They push it in and out as it goes in the skull. It just curls up and just smashes all the brain up here. And then obviously the other part of it is the bleeding of the animal. So the throat is cut and they're bled, over the blood bath. And then, once they're bled, they bring them round, and then start skinning them.

For the cattle, the shooting box was in the corner. And then the cattle race, that they used to come up into the shooting box, came from the lairage. I suppose the cattle race is about 25-30 feet long. So, the cattle in the race, and in the pens behind obviously, because of the nature of the building, they must have been able to hear what was going on. Obviously they'd be able to smell what was going on.

And most of them looked absolutely terrified, when they came into the shooting box. I used to say, "They know what's coming." Some of them would do anything to try and get out of that box, leaping up, trying to climb over the top. But they couldn't because it was too high.

Mr. Ingram recalls the reactions of outside people whenever they visited the facility.

We used to get people coming around the slaughterhouse. You know, groups of students, people who perhaps they were going to be vets or some other profession like that. And you could see the faces as soon as they walked into the slaughterhouse while the killing was going on. You could see them start to heave with the sights of all the blood and noise and everything else.

Surrounded by blood, urine, feces, pus, animal body parts and dismembered organs, these murderous jobs severely affect the workers' physical health. Between 2006 and 2008, 24 employees from two pig abattoirs in Indiana and Michigan, USA respectively fell ill with a paralyzing neurological disease. Each of these workers had been removing brains from pig skull cavities using highly compressed air.

Doctors later determined that the illness was caused by the inhalation of minute particles of pig brain tissue. Another serious problem is the devastating impact this violent environment has on the mental state of those involved in slaughterhouse operations. Jaylene Musgrave, who founded the Australian animal welfare organization Vegan Warriors, describes how her father, a slaughterhouse inspector, was profoundly affected by his job both physically and mentally.

He had to go and inspect the carcasses, to ensure that there were no diseases so that they were fit for human consumption. And this meant that quite often he was around animals that had been slaughtered where there were diseases, and that in turn made him sick. And he spent quite a lot of time in hospital being treated for the diseases that he'd picked up through that work.

Did it have any effect on his mental or psychological health as well as his physical health?

Yes, I truly believe it did, because he started to become quite an angry man. And I think it was having to deal with violence and death on a daily basis (which) really affected his psyche. And it came out in really bad ways. He started to drink very heavily. I don't know how he would go to sleep at night. And I think that's why he turned to drinking because it dulled the feelings that were inside of him.

There were a lot of men, because it was mainly men that worked there, that drank a lot. And unfortunately also that would turn to violence within the family home. And I do believe that has to do with what they had to go and do every single day. And I've thought about what impact it must have on them, going home knowing what they've done. So I suppose alcohol in those days definitely was very prevalent. And I would say today a lot of them would maybe even do drugs. You know, to cope with it, to try and blot it out.

Like Ms. Musgrave's father, Les Ingram and his fellow workers also tried to block out the stress and trauma from their jobs.

Well, I think a lot of the blokes in the industry used to deal with it with the help of alcohol. I used to go to the local football clubs after work every night; I'd be there until closing time. It's one way of dealing with what you've been dealing with all day; push it to the back of your mind. Go for a game of darts, game of cards, a few beers.

And I think a lot of blokes were only able to cope with the situation because of that. I mean in fact one of the slaughtermen that used to work there, every morning he'd have a fresh bottle of whisky. He used to nip in and out of the locker room, and that bottle of whisky would be gone during the course of the day.

Sometimes the behavior of abattoir employees manifests the madness that surrounds them at work. Les Ingram recalls one horrendous incident at the slaughterhouse.

They had a lot of ewes coming in at one particular point, and a lot of the ewes were actually in lamb and very close to having those lambs born. And so, of course, during the process of being slaughtered, the bags were taken out, and the lambs were inside the bags.

And there was one in particular quite big. And they opened the bag up

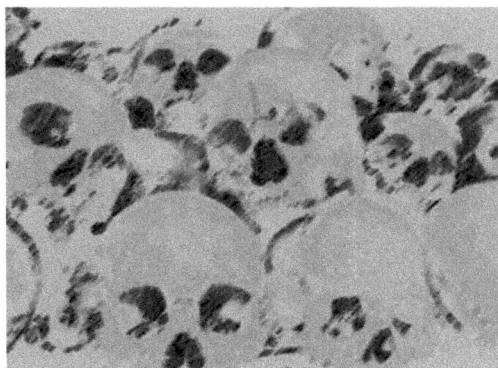

and took the lamb out and got some paper towels; wiped around her mouth, blew up her nose a few times, gave her a bit of a rub, and the lamb started breathing and was actually, alive and ready to go.

But this amused them for a few minutes and (then they) said, "Oh well, time to get on with the job." (They) just sssst, just cut (the lamb's) throat, just like that. They brought her to life out of the womb, got her going, and then just cut her throat. And that was just for amusement. That was the sort of thing that used to go on.

This same utter lack of caring and compassion has been seen in those who kill animals for a living outside the walls of meat processing facilities.

They become desensitized to what they're doing. I mean, anybody who can go up and hit a baby seal over the head is the same kind of mentality that'll go and stomp a kitten to death, you know? I find it completely unfathomable to see how anybody could do that, but I've

> *Why should man not be satisfied with grains, fruits and milk, which, combined together, can produce hundreds and thousands of palatable dishes. Why are there slaughterhouses all over the world to kill innocent animals? Maharaja Pariksit, grandson of Maharaja Yudhisthira, while touring his vast kingdom, saw a black man attempting to kill a cow. The King at once arrested the butcher and chastised him sufficiently. Should not a king or executive head protect the lives of the poor animals who are unable to defend themselves? Is this humanity? Are not the animals of a country citizens also? Then why are they allowed to be butchered in organized slaughterhouses? Are these the signs of equality, fraternity and nonviolence?*
>
> *Therefore, in contrast with the modern, advanced, civilized form of government, an autocracy like Maharaja Yudhisthira's is by far superior to a so-called democracy in which animals are killed and a man less than an animal is allowed to cast votes for another less-than-animal man.*
>
> *We are all creatures of material nature. In the Bhagavad-gita it is said that the Lord Himself is the seed-giving father and material nature is the mother of all living beings in all shapes. Thus mother material nature has enough foodstuff both for animals and for men, by the grace of the Father Almighty, Sri Krsna. The human being is the elder brother of all other living beings. He is endowed with intelligence more powerful than animals for realizing the course of nature and the indications of the Almighty Father.*
>
> ~ Srila Prabhupada (Srimad Bhagavatam 1.10.4)

seen them do it and they actually look on us as being strange that we don't partake of that.

The obscene violence shown towards animals in a slaughterhouse can also turn into violence towards fellow humans. Dr. Amy Fitzgerald, assistant professor of criminology at the University of Windsor, Canada, concluded that, in the United States, the link between slaughterhouses and murder, rape and other brutal crimes is an empirical fact, and that an average sized slaughterhouse with 175 employees increases the number of annual arrests in a community by 2.24 and the annual reports of violence by 4.69.

I really do feel that anyone involved in having to be hands-on in the taking of an animal's life, I think it does really get into the psychological aspect of a human being, and how they are in this world and how they walk around in this world. I've read of so many instances of people that have committed horrendous crimes towards people, serial killers and so forth. (They) have tortured animals on many occasions.

We lost the father that we knew, who was kind and gentle. And he became very angry at the world. And he became very, very violent and very aggressive towards my mom and towards us kids. And I really do think it was all because of what he was having to go through every day at work and being surrounded by the fear and the death.

Jaylene Musgrave's father's aggressiveness towards his family

An activist shooting a slaughterhouse scene

continued. Eventually he committed a violent crime and was sentenced to prison.

What was it that led to your father spending time in prison?

He actually couldn't cope with the stress at the time, and what was going through his head and his feelings. And he took it out on my mom. And, unfortunately we had a gun and he shot my mom. (It was) very fortunate that my mom didn't die, although she was disabled by it. So I know that my father, that evening after it had happened, went down to the river and put the gun in his mouth to take his own life, but he didn't go through with that. And that led to him being jailed.

I saw a lot of things I didn't like, that were absolutely shock... shocking. And they never, ever leave you. It's just like replaying a video Putting it on, you know, reverse, and then playing it back again and again and again. Because they never do leave you. I certainly wouldn't go back to anything like that. You know, even if it was the last job.

We pray that we soon live on a vegetarian planet, where such destructive and debilitating jobs no longer exist and all animals lead tranquil lives.

Reference

Supreme Master TV Series, 2011

Eisnitz, g. (1997). Slaughterhouse: The shocking story of greed, neglect, and inhumane treatment inside the U.S. meat industry. New York: Prometheus.

Beirne, P. (2004). From animal abuse to interhuman violence? A critical review of the progression thesis.

Society and Animals, 12, 39-65

15

School Shooters

Had Abused Animals First

W here does all the war, racism, terrorism, violence, and cruelty that's so endemic to human civilization come from? Why do humans exploit and massacre each other so regularly? Why is our species so violence-prone? To answer these questions we would do well to think about our exploitation and slaughter of animals and its effect on human civilization. Could it be that we oppress and kill each other so readily because our abuse and

slaughter of animals has desensitized us to the suffering and death of others?

Almost all the US schools shooters had a history of animal abuse. Some of them are described below:

April 1999/Littleton, Colo. Eric Harris and Dylan Klebold shot to death 12 fellow students and a teacher and injured more than 20 others. Both teens had reportedly boasted about mutilating animals.

May 1998/Springfield, Ore. Kip Kinkel, 15, killed his parents and opened fire in his high school cafeteria, killing two and injuring 22 others. He had a history of animal abuse and torture, having boasted about blowing up a cow and killing cats, chipmunks, and squirrels by putting lit firecrackers in their mouths.

March 1998/Jonesboro, Ark. Mitchell Johnson, 13, and Andrew Golden, 11, pulled their school's fire alarm and then shot and killed four classmates and a teacher. Golden reportedly used to shoot dogs "all the time with a .22."

> *tatas canu-dinam dharmah*
> *satyam saucam ksama daya*
> *kalena balina rajan*
> *nanksyaty ayur balam smrtih*
> Sukadeva Gosvami said: Then, O King, religion, truthfulness, cleanliness, tolerance, mercy, duration of life, physical strength and memory will all diminish day by day because of the powerful influence of the age of Kali.
> ~Srila Prabhupada (SB 12.2.1)

December 1997/West Paducah, Ky. Michael Carneal, 14, shot and killed three students during a school prayer meeting. Carneal had been heard talking about throwing a cat into a bonfire.

October 1997/Pearl, Miss. Luke Woodham, 16, shot and killed two of his classmates and injured seven others after stabbing his mother to death. Woodham's journal revealed that, in a moment of "true beauty," he and a friend had beaten, burned, and tortured his own dog, Sparkle, to death.

Reference

MS Treyce D'Gabriel-Montoya, Dangerous Ink, 1999, p123-125

Kawachi, I., Kennedy, B. P., & Wilkinson, R. g. (1999). Crime: Social disorganization and relative depravation.

Flynn, C. (2000a). Battered women and their animal companions: Symbolic interaction between human and non-human animals. Society and Animals, 8, 99-100

16

All In The Fray - Woman, Kids And Grannies

3 Year Olds To 90 Year Olds Join The War

He is barely old enough to go to infant school, let alone fight in a savage civil war.

Yet this youngster, believed to be just four years old, is one of the latest 'cub jihadists' recruited for bloody battle in Syria.

He can be seen firing rounds from an automatic assault rifle in a shocking video that has emerged from the war-torn country.

The youngster, who wears a black ski mask, can be seen firing shots from a black AK-47-style automatic assault rifle with a folding stock.

He is so small that the barrel of the gun has to be supported by a section of road block so that he can cope with its weight.

The child opens fire to shouts of Allahu Akbar – Arabic for 'God is Greater'.

Then there is another child. Puffing on a cigarette, a Kalashnikov AK-47 slung awkwardly across his little shoulders, seven-year-old Ahmed stands at a makeshift barricade in Syria. This is the image of a Syrian boy soldier with a thousand-yard stare.

He is one of the youngest fighters to be swept into his country's civil war and something in his blank expression seems to hint at horrors that no child of his age should ever have to witness.

The picture was taken in the neighbourhood of Salahadeen, one of the front lines in the battered city of Aleppo.

The son of a Free Syrian Army fighter, he is said to help operate a barricade that protects rebels from Syrian army snipers.

Ahmed seemed remarkably relaxed, his right hand and left elbow resting on the rifle, a pose likely to have been copied from the adult fighters around him.

It is thought hundreds of children have taken 'active roles' in the conflict, including running supplies and carrying messages between front-line units.

The photograph emerged as Samantha Cameron, on a visit to Syrian refugees in Lebanon, claimed innocent childhoods were being 'smashed to pieces' by the civil war.

The British Prime Minister's wife – an ambassador for Save the Children – said: 'It is horrifying to hear the harrowing stories from the children. No child should ever experience what they have.'

Last month, militant Khaled Sharrouf posted a Twitter image of his son, believed to be age seven, gripping the severed head of a Syrian soldier.

His father, a suspected war criminal, posted the photo alongside the caption: 'That's my boy!'.

Sisters In Arms Join The Fighting

As the Syrian uprising drags into its third year, women are taking an increasingly active role in the conflict, on both sides.

For the regime of President Bashar al-Assad, a women's militia — officially dubbed "Lionesses" — is guarding checkpoints and running security operations in support of the army. On the rebel side, women are smuggling weapons, sometimes fighting alongside the men, and even forming their own brigades.

"We see women rebels fighting in the Kurdish areas, in Aleppo, in Homs," said Rami Abdul-Rahman, founder of the Syrian Observatory for Human Rights, a monitoring group based in Britain. Women are holding positions both on the battlefront and behind the lines, he said.

This reflects a new strand in the Syrian civil war, according to commanders, opposition politicians, journalists, aid workers and activists. Women on both sides are seeking a bigger military role and are finding ways around cultural barriers that keep them from the battlefield.

"Without a doubt, there are many more involved," Mr. Abdul-Rahman said. He said an estimated 5,000 revolutionary women were now engaged in fighting and military logistics, though the exact number is difficult to know because of the dangerous and chaotic situation.

A senior commander of the Free Syrian Army, who agreed to speak on condition that he not be named, confirmed that several women's brigades had been formed in recent months. He said that the regime was doing the same.

Women of all ages and social backgrounds have become involved in activities ranging from cooking for fighters to running complex and dangerous operations, according to rebel military commanders and media reports.

Disciple: If we look back over this century, Srila Prabhupada, we can't find many years of peace. The Russo-Japanese War, the First World War, the Second World War. the Korean War, the Vietnam War, and hundreds of what they call "low-intensity conflicts." But always some kind of war going on. Whether in the Middle East or Latin America or Africa, people are always fighting over land and industrial resources. It seems some kind of war always has to be going on.

Srila Prabhupada: Yes, always some war. "Cold war" or "hot war," as they say. When there is the fire of physical combat that is a hot war. And when there are diplomacy and politics, that is a cold war. So war is going on. Sometimes it is hot; sometimes it is cold. There is no peace.

~ Srila Prabhupada (Conversation, New Vrindaban. West Virginia, June 26, 1976.)

Various media, including Al Jazeera and The Daily Telegraph, have reported on the activities of women rebel snipers, notably in the strife-torn city of Aleppo.

Kurdish women have been fighting on numerous fronts — with the rebels, with pro-regime forces and with separatist militias — for some time, the observatory said. Five Kurdish women's brigades are currently operating, it said.

The regime "is killing children and women and doesn't differentiate between men, women, children or the elderly, so that's why we are willing to go side by side with the men in the battlefield," says a woman fighter.

In January the regime began a recruitment drive for the "Lionesses for National Defense," a militia force deploying women volunteers to carry out security operations, control checkpoints and free up soldiers to fight.

Lee Worton how horrible. we have a slaughterhouse in a town about 1 1/2 hours from me and you can smell death when you come near it going down the highway. I usually try and take a detour around that place whenever I have to go past the city. And when I see the trucks loaded with those poor animals going there, all I can do is say a prayer for them. Slaughtered animals were main #1 reason of me becoming a vegetarian over 40 years ago. and then I went into doing rescue of abandoned animals.

Gran's Army - Grannies Take Up Kalashnikovs

In the strategic town of Kobani and several other places, grannies have taken up Kalashnikovs to defend their towns. As they witness

brutal killing of their family members, they say they have no other option but to take up the arms. The militants are unleashing a rein of terror in the areas they occupy. There are summary executions and girls are having their hearts cut out after brutal gang rapes.

Meanwhile in Afganistan, a grieving Afghan mother takes bloody revenge by killing 25 Taliban militants during seven hour battle after they gunned down her son

Reza Gul watched helplessly as her son died while he manned a village checkpoint with his small team of police officers in the lawless Farah province.

But flanked by her daughter and daughter-in-law, she led a counter strike on his attackers killing 25 militants and wounding

another five during a ferocious seven hour gun battle.

Her daughter-in-law Seema added: 'The fighting was intensified when we reached the battlefield along with light and heavy weapons. We were committed to fight until the last bullet.'

She added that the combats zone was strewn with Taliban bodies when the fighting was over.

Alongside other insurgent groups, the Taliban have escalated attacks across the country since the withdrawal of most of the US led forces from the country last month.

Targeting, government, security and foreign installations, especially in the country's capital Kabul, members of the public have also been caught in the crossfire.

Source
David Williams, Daily Mail, 28 March 2013
Sam Greenhill, The Daily Mail, 6 October 2014
ABC News, Inside Kobani: Kurdish Women On The Frontline
Kobani, Syria — Dec 2, 2014
Henry Austin, The Daily Mail, 26 November 2014 |

17

Violence begets violence

The phrase "violence begets violence" means that violent behavior promotes other violent behavior, in return. The phrase has been used for over 50 years, as in speeches by Dr. Martin Luther King, Jr. (1958)[1] or the news report "Study: TV Violence Begets Violence" by CBS News (March 2003).[2]

Violence begets violence and evil begets evil are concepts described in the Gospel of Matthew, verse 26:52.[3] The passage depicts a disciple (identified in the Gospel of John as Peter) drawing

a sword to defend against the arrest of Jesus but being told to sheath his weapon:

Then said Jesus unto him, Put up again thy sword into his place: for all they that take the sword shall perish with the sword.[4]

Words by Dr. King[edit]

The reverend Martin Luther King, Jr. (1929-1968) used the phrase when saying:[1][5][6]

Hate begets hate; violence begets violence; toughness begets a greater toughness. We must meet the forces of hate with the power of love... Our aim must never be to defeat or humiliate the white man, but to win his friendship and understanding.[1]

"The ultimate weakness of violence is that it is a descending spiral begetting the very thing it seeks to destroy, instead of diminishing evil, it multiplies it.

Through violence you may murder the liar, but you cannot murder the lie, nor establish the truth.

Through violence you may murder the hater, but you do not murder hate. In fact, violence merely increases hate.

Returning violence for violence multiplies violence, adding deeper darkness to a night already devoid of stars.

Darkness cannot drive out darkness; only light can do that.

Hate cannot drive out hate; only love can do that."

References

Wikipedia, 1. "Struggle for Equality: Quotes From Martin Luther King, Jr.", Scholastic Inc., January 2011, webpage: [1].

2. Study: TV Violence Begets Violence", CBS News, 10 March 2003, webpage: CBS-33.

3. Tesh, S. Edward; Walter D. Zorn. Psalms, Volume 1. p. 291.

4. Matthew 26:52, King James Version.

5. Stride Toward Freedom: The Montgomery Story, Martin Luther King, Jr., Clayborne Carson, 2010 (256 pages), page 74, ISBN 0-8070-0069-8, web: Books-Google-YC.

6. "Dr. Martin Luther King Jr. Community Celebration - Quotes" WSU.edu, January 30, 2011, webpage: WSU-481.

18

Facts About Animal Abuse

And Domestic Violence

These excerpts are from a report published by National Coalition Against Domestic Violence, USA.

Why it Matters

71% of pet-owning women entering women's shelters reported that their batterer had injured, maimed, killed or threatened family pets for revenge or to psychologically control victims; 32% reported their children had hurt or killed animals.

68% of battered women reported violence towards their animals. 87% of these incidents occurred in the presence of the women, and 75% in the presence of the children, to psychologically control and coerce them.

13% of intentional animal abuse cases involve domestic violence.

Between 25% and 40% of battered women are unable to escape abusive situations because they worry about what will happen to their pets or livestock should they leave.

Pets may suffer unexplained injuries, health problems, permanent disabilities at the hands of abusers, or disappear from home.

Abusers kill, harm, or threaten children's pets to coerce them into sexual abuse or to force them to remain silent about abuse. Disturbed children kill or harm animals to emulate their parents' conduct, to prevent the abuser from killing the pet, or to take out their aggressions on another victim.

In one study, 70% of animal abusers also had records for other crimes. Domestic violence victims whose animals were abused saw the animal cruelty as one more violent episode in a long history of indiscriminate violence aimed at them and their vulnerability.

Investigation of animal abuse is often the first point of social services intervention for a family in trouble.

For many battered women, pets are sources of comfort providing strong emotional support: 98% of Americans consider pets to be companions or members of the family.

Animal cruelty problems are people problems. When animals are abused, people are at risk.

Did You Know?

More American households have pets than have children. They spend more money on pet food than on baby food. There are more dogs in the U.S. than people in most countries in Europe - and more cats than dogs.

A child growing up in the U.S. is more likely to have a pet than a live-at-home father.

Pets live most frequently in homes with children: 64.1% of homes with children under age 6, and 74.8% of homes with children over

age 6, have pets. The woman is the primary caregiver in 72.8% of pet-owning households.

Battered women have been known to live in their cars with their pets for as long as four months until an opening was available at a pet-friendly safe house.

Source

[1] Ascione, F.R., Weber, C. V. & Wood, D. S. (1997). The abuse of animals and domestic violence: A national survey of shelters for women who are battered. Society & Animals 5(3), 205-218.

[2] Quinlisk, J.A. (1999). Animal Abuse and Family Violence. In, Ascione, F.R. & Arkow, P., eds.: Child Abuse, Domestic Violence, and Animal Abuse: Linking the Circles of Compassion for Prevention and Intervention. West Lafayette, IN: Purdue University Press, pp. 168-175.

[3] Humane Society of the U.S. (2001). 2000 Report of Animal Cruelty Cases. Washington, DC.

[4] Arkow, P. (2003). Breaking the cycles of violence: A guide to multi-disciplinary interventions. A handbook for child protection, domestic violence and animal protection agencies. Alameda, CA: Latham Foundation.

[5] McIntosh, S. (2001). Calgary research results: Exploring the links between animal abuse and domestic violence. The Latham Letter 22(4), 14-16.

[6] Arkow, P. (1994). Animal abuse and domestic violence: Intake statistics tell a sad story. Latham Letter 15(2), 17.

[7] Jorgensen, S. & Maloney, L. (1999). Animal abuse and the victims of domestic violence. In, F.R. Ascione & P. Arkow, eds.: Child Abuse, Domestic Violence, and Animal Abuse: Linking the Circles of Compassion for Prevention and Intervention. West Lafayette, IN: Purdue University Press, pp. 143-158.

19

Terror deaths 'jumped sharply in 2013'

According to the Institute for Economics and Peace, the number of people killed globally in terrorist attacks jumped by 61 percent in 2013, reflecting the rise of Boko Haram and Islamic State jihadists.

In its 2014 Global Terrorism Index launched in London, the Australian based research group reported there were almost 10,000 terrorist attacks in 2013, a 44 percent increase from 2012.

These attacks resulted in 17,958 fatalities, up from 11,133 in 2012, with over 80 percent of the deaths occurring in just five countries: Iraq, Afghanistan, Pakistan, Nigeria and Syria.

Iraq was found to be the country most affected by terrorism, recording a 164 percent rise in fatalities, to 6362, with IS responsible for most of the deaths.

Four groups: IS, Boko Haram, al-Qaeda and the Taliban were blamed for 66 percent of all fatalities.

On the street, in your front, if somebody's being killed, nobody will take care; he'll go on. There is no mercifulness. Even the mother has no mercifulness, killing the child. This is Kali-yuga.

-Srila Prabhupada (Srimad-Bhagavatam 7.6.3 -Toronto, June 19, 1976)

But the report found that attacks had also increased in the rest of the world, with fatalities rising by half the previous figure, to 3236 in 2013.

A total of 60 countries recorded deaths from terrorist attacks last year.

"Since we first launched the GTI in 2012, we've seen a significant and worrying increase in worldwide incidences of terrorism," said Steve Killelea, Executive Chairman of IEP.

"Over the last decade the increase in terrorism has been linked to radical Islamic groups whose violent theologies have been broadly taught. To counteract these influences, moderate forms of Sunni theologies need to be championed by Sunni Muslim nations," he added.

Killelea urged leaders to reduce state-sponsored violence, reduce group grievances and improve community-supported policing to reduce the threat.

The report highlighted Angola, Bangladesh, Burundi, Central African Republic, Ivory Coast, Ethiopia, Iran, Israel, Mali, Mexico, Myanmar, Sri Lanka and Uganda as countries at increased risk from terror attacks.

Despite the global spike, the report stressed that the risk to westerners remained slim.

According to its figures, a person in Britain was 188 times more likely to be victim of a murder, and in the US 64 times more likely, than a terrorist attack.

Reference

Voice of America, November 18 2014, James Pheby

Reuters, The Telegraph, November 19 , 2014

IOL News, November 18 2014

20

Senseless Violence of A Desensitized Generation

Baseball Player Killed By "Bored" Oklahoma Teens

After Killing An Animal, They Didn't Have Anything Else To Do, So They Decided To Kill Somebody.

A random act of violence left a promising 23-year-old college baseball player dead, a family devastated and two countries half a world apart rattled.

Christopher Lane, who was from Australia, was gunned down in Duncan, Oklahoma, while he was out jogging in August 2013. The motive? Three teens who had nothing better to do, according to police.

"They witnessed a young man run by on the street. Chose him as the target," Police Chief Danny Ford told CNN.

James Edwards Jr., 15, and Chancey Luna, 16, were charged as adults with felony

The Victim

murder in the first degree, according to Kaylee Chandler, Stephens County Court Clerk.

Michael Jones, 17, faces two charges -- use of a vehicle in the discharge of a weapon and accessory after the fact to murder in the first degree, she said.

A judge set bond at $1 million for Jones, while no bond was set for Edwards and Luna, Chandler said.

When police arrested the teens, one of them offered up a motive that made clear that Lane, who attended East Central University on a baseball scholarship, was chosen at random.

"He said the motive was, 'We were going to kill somebody.'" "They decided all three of them were going to kill somebody."

A brutal crime

Police say the teens shot Lane in the back in the town of about 24,000 and sped away in their car.

"There were some people that saw him stagger across the road, go to a kneeling position and collapse on the side of the road," Ford told CNN.

Attempts to revive Lane failed.

Police caught the teens a few hours after the shooting. Thanks to security cameras from local businesses, police saw their car speeding down the street. Lane was remembered as magnetic -- the sort of

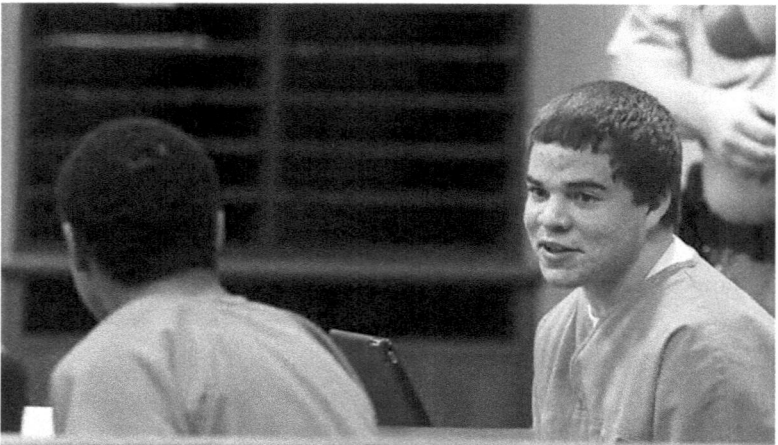

Killers laughing in court with no remorse

person who could always lighten the mood. "Chris was a charming guy, genuinely good person, with great character and had a love for life. As cliché as it sounds Chris was the kind of guy you want your sons to grow up to be and that you want your daughters to marry. It just breaks my heart knowing how much more he could have brought to this world as a husband, father, son, brother and friend," said Sam Malchar, a former ECU teammate and classmate.

Half a world away

Nearly 10,000 miles away in Australia, Lane's family struggled to cope with the news.

"He's left his mark as we know, and you know there's not going to be any good come out of this, because it was just so senseless," Christopher's father, Peter Lane, said. "It's happened. It's wrong, and we're just trying and deal with it the best we can."

Lane's girlfriend, Sarah Harper, posted an emotional tribute on Facebook, saying "you will always be mine and in a very special and protected place in my heart."

Friends and strangers alike posted condolences on another Facebook page, honoring the slain baseball player. "Such a sad waste of a young man's life," one poster wrote. "Know that many Americans are sorry for this tragedy and want justice for Chris," wrote another. "God bless."

....When we lose respect for animal life, we lose respect for human life as well. Twenty-six hundred years ago, Pythagoras said, "Those that kill animals to eat their flesh tend to massacre their own." We're fearful of enemy guns, bombs, and missiles, but can we close our eyes to the pain and fear we ourselves bring about by slaughtering, for human consumption, over 1.6 billion domestic mammals and 22.5 billion poultry a year. The number of fish killed each year is in the trillions. And what ot speak of the tens of millions of animals killed each year in the "torture-camps" of medical research laboratories, or slaughtered for their fur, hide, or skin, or hunted for "sport". Can we deny that this brutality makes us more brutal too?"

~ Adiraja Dasa (The Hare Krishna Book of Vegetarian Cooking)

Police told CNN the suspects may have killed an animal prior to shooting Lane, and that they planned on killing more people.

Senseless Violence On The Rise

Senseless Violence is a term frequently used by among others the media, politicians and NGOs to define the nature of several shocking events in the world in recent years. The term expresses the perceived senselessness of the occurred acts of violence.

For example, a series of uncoordinated mass stabbings, hammer attacks, and cleaver attacks on school children in the People's Republic of China began in March 2010. The spate of attacks left at least 25 dead and some 115 injured. Most cases had no known motive. Following are some of the cases:

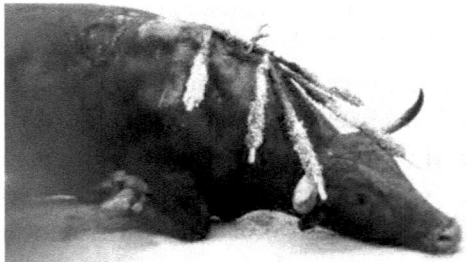

On March 23, 2010, Zheng Minsheng 41, murdered eight children with a knife in an elementary school in Nanping, Fujian province.

In April 2010, just a few hours after the execution of Zheng Minsheng in neighboring Fujian Province, in Leizhou, Guangdong another knife-wielding man named Chen Kangbing, 33 at Hongfu Primary School wounded 16 students and a teacher.

On April 29 in Taixing, Jiangsu, 47-year-old Xu Yuyuan went to Zhongxin Kindergarten and stabbed 28 students and two teachers after stabbing the security guard. Most of the Taixing students were 4 years old. The attack was the second in China in just two days.

On April 30, Wang Yonglai used a hammer to cause head injury to preschool children in Weifang, Shandong, then used gasoline to commit suicide by self-immolation.

An attacker named Wu Huanming, 48, killed seven children and two adults and injured 11 other persons with a cleaver at a kindergarten in Hanzhong, Shaanxi on May 12, 2010.

On May 18, 2010 at Hainan Institute of Science and Technology, a vocational college in Haikou, Hainan, more than 10 men charged into a dormitory wielding knives around 2:30 am; after attacking the security guard and disabling security cameras, 9 students were injured, 1 seriously.

On 4 August 2010, 26-year-old Fang Jiantang slashed more than 20 children and staff with a 60 cm knife, killing 3 children and 1 teacher, at a kindergarten in Zibo, Shandong province. There was no known motive. Since the start of the year, a total of 27 people had died and at least 80 were injured in various knife attacks.

In August 2011, eight children, all aged four or five, were hurt in Minhang District, Shanghai when an employee at a child-care centre for migrant workers slashed the children who were 3 to 4 years old with a box-cutter.

In September 2011, a young girl and three adults taking their children to nursery school were killed in Gongyi, Henan by 30-year-old Wang Hongbin with an axe.

On 14 December 2012, a 36 year-old villager in the village of Chenpeng, Henan Province, stabbed 23 children and an elderly woman at the village's primary school as children were arriving for classes.

Reference

By Ed Payne and Elizabeth Stuart, CNN, August 21, 2013

Associated Press And Daily Mail Reporter, 20 March 2014

"China knife attack 'kills eight'". BBC News. 9 May 2010.

China-xian.com. 15 December 2012.

Students In China Stabbed In Elementary School Attack by 36-year-old Villager Min Yongjun". American Live Wire. Retrieved 15 December 2012.

Evan Osnos (15 December 2012). "China Watches Newtown: Guns and American Credibility". The New Yorker.

McAuliff, Michael (15 December 2012). "On Gun Control, Jerry Nadler Explains What Congress Could Do Right Now". The Huffington Post.

Hutzler, Charles (15 December 2012). "Schools and students are targets worldwide". Associated Press. Retrieved 15 December 2012.

Bodeen, christopher (May 12, 2010). "9 killed in latest attack at China school". Associated Press.

FlorCruz, Jaime (May 3, 2010). "Execution does not stop Chinese knife attacks". CNN.

Canaves, Sky (April 30, 2010). "Knife Attacks Plague Schools in China". Wall Street Journal.

21

Modern Conflicts: Dizzying Acts Of Brutality

A Modern Mall Turns Into A Slaughterhouse

'Eyes Gouged Out, Bodies Hanging From Hooks, And Fingers Removed With Pliers'

O n 21 September 2013, unidentified gunmen attacked the upmarket Westgate shopping mall in Nairobi, Kenya. The attack, which lasted until 24 September, resulted in at least 67 deaths, including four attackers. Over 175 people were reportedly wounded in the mass shooting, with all of the gunmen reported killed.

The Islamist group al-Shabaab claimed responsibility for the incident.

The country was celebrating the International Day of Peace when the incident took place.

Soldiers told of the horrific torture meted out by terrorists wherein hostages were dismembered, had their eyes gouged out and were left hanging from hooks in the ceiling.

Men were said to have been castrated and had fingers removed with pliers before being blinded and hanged.

Children were found dead in the food court fridges with knives still embedded in their bodies.

Most of the terrorists were reportedly discovered 'burnt to ashes', set alight by the last extremist standing to try to protect their identities.

The horrifying details came as the pictures emerged from within the wreckage of the building, showing piles of bodies left strewn across the floor.

> *"Sometimes they kill the animal simply, and it throbs and suffers in a pool of blood. They like that. So the hunters, some of the hunters, they also kill the animal half. So they take pleasure. I have seen in my own eyes in Calcutta. One hotel man was cutting the throat of a chicken and half-cut, and the half-dead chicken was jumping like this, and the man was laughing. His little son, he was crying. I have seen it. He was crying. Because he's innocent child, he could not tolerate. He was crying. And the father was saying, "Why you are crying? Why you are crying? It is very nice." Just see. So without being devotee a man will become cruel, cruel, cruel, cruel, cruel, in this way go to hell. And devotee cannot tolerate. We have studied in the life of Lord Jesus Christ. When he saw that in the Jewish synagogue the birds were being killed, he became shocked. He therefore left. Jesus... He inaugurated the Christian religion. Perhaps you know. He was shocked by this animal-killing. And therefore his first commandment is "Thou shall not kill." But the foolish Christians, instead of following his instruction, they are opening daily slaughterhouse."*
>
> *~ Srila Prabhupada (Lecture on Srimad-Bhagavatam, 04-07-76, Vrindavan)*

A third of the mall was destroyed in the battle between terrorists and Kenyan troops.

Even the doctors who were among the first people into the mall after it was reclaimed, spoke of the horrifying scenes inside.

'You find people with hooks hanging from the roof,' said one Kenyan doctor, who asked not to be named.

'They removed eyes, ears, nose. They get your hand and sharpen it like a pencil then they tell you to write your name with the blood.

'They drive knives inside a child's body.

'Actually if you look at all the bodies, unless those ones that were escaping, fingers are cut by pliers, the noses are ripped by pliers. Here it was pain.'

A soldier, who took pictures at a bread counter and at the ArtCaffe, said he was so traumatised by what he saw he has had to seek counselling.

Children's buggies were left abandoned just metres from the yawning pit, as cars hang precariously over the edge. Beneath many more vehicles lie on top of each other, smashed to pieces.

During the firefight, hostages reportedly had their throats slashed from ear to ear and were thrown screaming from third-floor balconies as the siege came to a bloody end.

Shell-shocked Kenyan troops said the inside of the Israeli-run mall resembled a 'scene from a horror movie' with blood spattered everywhere and dead bodies strewn across the floor.

One soldier told the Daily Mirror: 'I have seen many bad things, but this will haunt me for the rest of my days.'

One massacre survivor smeared herself in the blood of a teenage victim to make gunmen think she was dead

Reference

Paul Bentley, The Daily Mail, 26 September 2013.

Blair, Edmund (21 September 2013). "Islamists claim gun attack on Nairobi mall, at least 39 dead". Reuters, 22 September 2013.

Jason Straziuso (December 13, 2013). "NYPD report on Kenya attack isn't US gov't view". Associated Press, Yahoo News. March 18, 2014.

"Kenyan military frees most hostages at mall". Raidió Teilifís Éireann. 23 Sept 2013.

22

When An Animal Abuser

Becomes A National Leader

As discussed in the previous chapters, there is a direct link between the way a person treats animals and the way he treats his fellow human beings.

This trait assumes significance when the animal abuser becomes a national leaders. As a kid, George Bush, former President of US, enjoyed putting firecrackers into frogs, throwing them in the air, and then watching them blow up. Should this be cause for alarm? How relevant is a man's childhood behavior to what he is like as an adult? Can we link this childhood behaviour of his with the heavy bloodshed and so called wars on terrorism during his tenure.

Cruelty to animals is a common precursor to later criminal violence. In fact, Bush's childhood friend, Terry Throckmorton,

Bush's best moment in office? Catching fish!

Agencies
BERLIN

US PRESIDENT George W Bush told a German newspaper that his best moment in more than five years in office was catching a big perch in his own lake. "You know, I've experi-

enced many great moments and it's hard to name the best," Bush told weekly Bild am Sonntag when asked about his high point since becoming president in January '01. "I would say the best moment of all was when I caught a 7.5 pound (3.402 kilos) perch in my lake," he told the

newspaper in an interview published on Sunday. Bush said the worst moment was September 11 when hijacked planes crashed into the World Trade Center in New York and the Pentagon in Washington. "It takes a while before one understands what is happening," he said.

openly and laughingly admits, "We were terrible to animals. A dip behind the Bush borne turned into a small lake after a good rain, and thousands of frogs would come out. We would get BB guns and shoot them, Or we'd put firecrackers in the frogs and throw them and blow them up."

So how much importance should we attribute to this early behavior?

Is boy George's lack of empathy and cruelty not just childhood insensitivity, but rather a personality trait still present in the man? If so, we have much to be concerned about. Do we really want a man who appears to be empathetically challenged to hold the most powerful position in a country like America?

We don't say, "Don't eat." You are so very fond of eating cows. All right, you can eat them, because after their death we have to give them to somebody, some living entity. Generally, cow carcasses are given to the vultures. But then, why only to the vultures? Why not to the modern "civilized" people, who are as good as vultures? [Laughter.]

These so-called civilized people--what is the difference between these rascals and vultures? The vultures also enjoy killing and then eating the dead body. "Make it dead and then enjoy"--people have become vultures. And their civilization is a vulture civilization. Animal-eaters--they're like jackals, vultures, dogs. Flesh is not proper food for human beings. Here in the Vedic culture is civilized food, human food: milk, fruit, vegetables, nuts, grains. Let them learn it. Uncivilized rogues, vultures, raksasas [demons]--and they're leaders.

Therefore I say that today the leaders are all fourth-class men. And that is why the whole world is in a chaotic condition. We require learned spiritual teachers--first-class men--to lead. What is the use of fourth-class men leading a confused and chaotic society?

If I speak so frankly, people will be very angry. But basically, their leaders are all fourth class. First-class men are great devotees of the Lord, who can guide the administrators and the citizens through their words and practical example.

~ Srila Prabhupada (Conversation - Valencey, France, June 1974)

Reference

Animal People, July/August 2000, p. 18.

http://www.all-creatures.org/aip/nl-3nov2000-frogs.html

Daily Kos, Aug 02, 2004, Bush Blew Up Frogs

23

Horrors of A Needless War

A Young Woman's Heart-rending Appeal To Bomb Her

The numerical phrase, 9/11 and the catch-all phrase "war on terror" have repeatedly been recited and relied on by the Bush administration to justify military action in Afghanistan and Iraq as well as the imposition of other draconian measures on some of its own citizens, e.g. the Patriot Act, and other homeland security measures. However, it has now been clearly demonstrated in all manner of ways, and even by Bush's belated grudging acknowledgment – that before the US invasion of Iraq there was no training of, or support for terrorists in Iraq; that Iraq was not intent on attacking the US. WMDs (Weapons of Mass Destruction) non-existence speaks volumes about a lying and deceptive US administration. The term "terrorism" has now become a fashionable tool or a tactic that some unscrupulous countries are now using, taking their cue from the US, to crush or suppress any legitimate dissent or opposition within or outside their borders.

Consider these statements: -

"Hussein has not developed any significant capability with respect to weapons of mass destruction. He is unable to project conventional power against his neighbors."

–Colin Powell on February 24, 2001

"Simply stated, there is no doubt that Saddam Hussein now has weapons of mass destruction,"

–Dick Cheney on August 26, 2002.

"Our conservative estimate is that Iraq today has a stockpile of between 100 and 500 tons of chemical weapons agent. That is enough agent to fill 16,000 battlefield rockets. Even the low   end of 100 tons of agent would enable Saddam Hussein to cause mass casualties across more than 100 square miles of territory, an area nearly five times the size of Manhattan."

–Colin Powell at the UN on February 5, 2003

"Intelligence leaves no doubt that Iraq continues to possess and conceal lethal weapons."

–George W. Bush on March 18, 2003

"We are asked to accept Saddam decided to destroy those weapons. I say that such a claim is palpably absurd."

–Tony Blair, Prime Minister 18 March 2003

"Saddam's removal is necessary to eradicate the threat from his weapons of mass destruction."

–Jack Straw, British Foreign Secretary 2 April 2003

"Before people crow about the absence of weapons of mass destruction, I suggest they wait a bit."

–Tony Blair 28 April, 2003

These facts can not leave any sensible and rational person in doubt about the levels of dishonesty, collusion, fabrication and calculated deception that led the invasion of Iraq in 2003.

Decision makers in the US bombed, invaded, occupied and caused at lowest estimate over 1,25,000 innocent civilian deaths in Iraq's oil war. Many more have died indirectly, from the loss of clean drinking water, healthcare, and nutrition. An additional 365,000 have been wounded and 7.8 million people have been displaced.

These are the human consequences of the way in which powerful interests pursue the ends of dominance over global oil supplies.

US cost of war in the last one decade alone has been $3.7 trillion and counting. Those numbers will continue to soar when considering often overlooked costs such as long-term obligations to wounded veterans and projected war spending from 2012 through 2020. The estimates do not include at least $1 trillion more in interest payments coming due and many billions more in expenses that cannot be counted, according to the study.

Questions are being raised as to what the United States gained from its multitrillion-dollar investment. Millions are living a life of perpetual misery in this lawless region. ISIS, a radical group now controls vast swathes of land here.

Now A Young Woman Seeks More Bombs

A young Yazidi woman forced into sex slavery by the ISIS begged

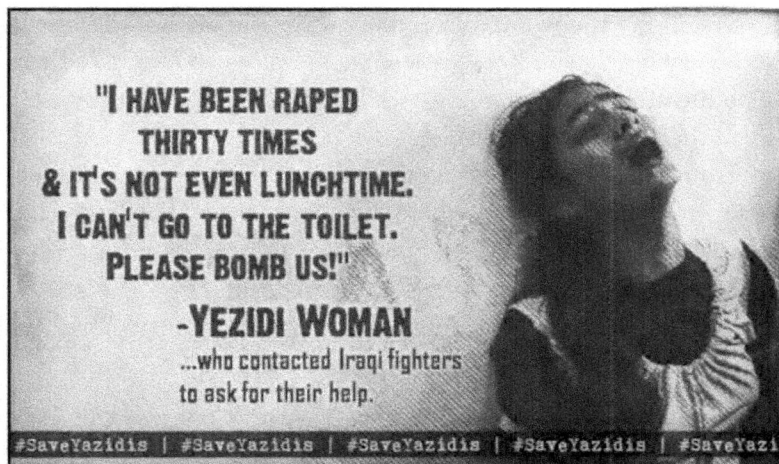

the West to bomb the brothel where she was being held after ISIS militants her 30 times in just a few hours. The unidentified

And Bernard Shaw, I think, he wrote one book, "You Are What You Eat."
Hamsadūta: George Bernard Shaw.
Prabhupāda: Yes. So they are becoming animals, animals eating animal flesh.
(Room Conversation -- December 13, 1970, Indore)

woman is understood to have been kept as a prisoner of the jihadists somewhere in western Iraq having been captured by ISIS during the Sinjar massacre in early August.

A group raising awareness of ISIS' persecution of women in the vast swathes of the Middle East under its control said the woman had contacted Kurdish peshmerga fighters by telephone to plead for the brothel to be bombed to put the women held as sex slaves out of their misery.

She allegedly told the fighters she had been raped so frequently by the ISIS militants that she could no longer use the toilet, adding that the ordeal has been so harrowing that she plans to commit suicide even if freed.

A man identified as Karam described how a friend embedded with the peshmerga took a phone call from the Yazidi woman.

Describing the woman as crying on the phone, Karam quoted her as saying: 'If you know where we are please bomb us... There is no life after this. I'm going to kill myself anyway - others have killed themselves this morning.'

Around 5-7,000 Yazidi women are being held in makeshift detention centres by ISIS, where they either been taken away and sold into slavery or handed over to jihadists as concubines.

Recently the UN confirmed that thousands of Yazidis were slaughtered in scenes reminiscent of the Bosnian Srebrenica massacre when ISIS swept through northern Iraq in August.

The Iraqi Children 'Drinking Their Parents' Blood To Stay Alive'

Children trapped on a mountain by Islamic State militants in Iraq were drinking blood from their parents to stay alive.

Their horrendous plight was revealed after some 8,000 Yazidis were finally able to escape down Mount Sinjar where they had been under siege from jihadist fighters in August 2014.

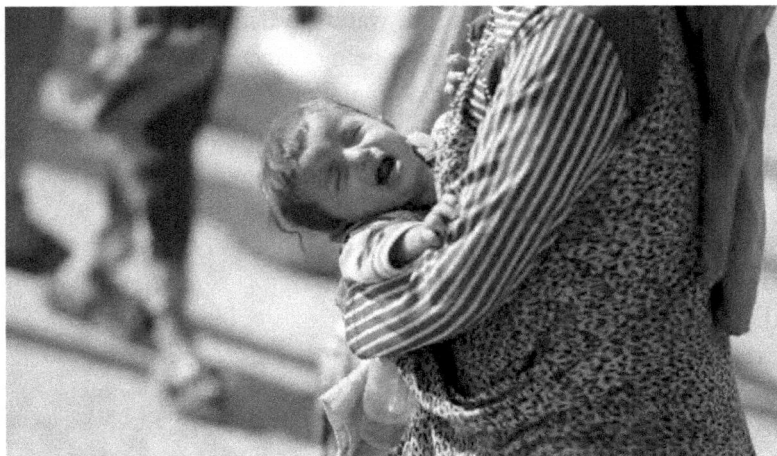

Those fleeing made it to relative safety at a camp in Dohuk Province in Kurdistan, where they told horrific stories of the 30,000 who had been left behind.

Sky News correspondent Sherine Tadros, who was at the camp, said: 'One man has just told us how he saw four children die of thirst.

'There was nowhere to bury them on the mountain so they just put rocks on their bodies.

'Another man was saying the children were so thirsty, their parents started cutting their own hands and giving them blood to drink.'

Hundreds of other families also made it across the border after trekking for hundreds of kilometres through sweltering temperatures to safety

They were being given food, water and medical treatment at shelters in Turkey and Syria after being driven out of their town.

Some have been forced to pay smugglers their life savings to take them on perilous journeys across the border into Turkey, sometimes through minefields.

They are among several gruelling treks to freedom the community has taken after they were sent scattering to the four corners by the insurgency, which has trapped around 30,000 others on Sinjar Mountain with no food or water.

One mother who suffers agonising rheumatism told how she and her three young children waded through the Tigris River, tip-toed her way through a minefield and climbed through a barbed-wire fence to make it into Turkey.

A prime example is the Middle East, where destiny has embroiled Christians, Moslems, and Jews -- the world's "religious" meat-eaters -- in a perennial paradigm of hatred and war. The peoples to whom the Lord delivered the Old Testament, New Testament, and Koran are always reinterpreting His words to suit their appetites. Now, "Thou shall not kill," conveniently reads, "Thou shall not commit murder," and the Moslem's and the Jew's "ritual slaughter" of fully conscious cows turns out to be more cruel than the "humane" stun-killing of the Christian. But the Lord is pleased with neither. And war in the Middle East -- and everywhere else -- continues.

~ Suresvara dasa, You Can Talk of Peace Till the Cows Come Home

Half-way through the five-hour journey, Amal said the smuggler wanted her children to leave her behind because she was too slow, but they chose to carry her instead.

The 43-year-old told The Times: 'My sons gathered around me and they refused. We were not afraid of dying there. We were afraid of dying at the hands of the Islamic State.'

Another teenager has not been so lucky.

I'm not a vegetarian and have no intention of giving up meat. Its just that I've been watching this documentary about horror films while eating ribs. And it occurred to me that we are horrified by human gore, yet we kill and eat animals all the time without feeling bad about it because we are so used it; its weird that double standard. And its also funny how we view animals differently.

And I hate to admit this, but the other day I went to a country park with some family and the whole time I was very hungry. And I stood watching these ducks in a lake and admiring the way the light reflected off the lake, and the trails of water left in the wake of the ducks floating around, and I was thinking to myself that this scene would have made a nice painting. When all of a sudden something crossed my mind. Lately I have got into buying duck breasts from the supermarket and having duck roast dinners.

In the past I always viewed ducks as a cute ornamental bird, however now all of a sudden I viewed them differently as like a floating duck breast. One of the ducks was within arms reach and for a second the thought of snatching one crossed my mind. Not that I would ever ever do something like that but you know. And my aunty then called me over and we went for lunch in this very nice restaurant.

We act all civilised and everything, but we are quite savage really aren't we?

~ Bill Lewis, Lakewood, Colorado

Amer Omar Pajo said he watched his father get shot in the head by gunmen as they fled to the mountains and his mother later succumbed to dehydration.

Iraq Crisis : Acts Of Inhumanity On Unimaginable Scale - UN

The UN says it has received reports from Iraq that "reveal acts of inhumanity on an unimaginable scale".

Deputy Human Rights Commissioner Flavia Pansieri said Islamic State (IS) was believed to have committed systematic and intentional attacks on civilians.

They include targeted killings, forced conversions, slavery, sexual

abuse, and the besieging of entire communities.

The UN Human Rights Council agreed to send an emergency mission to investigate the IS crimes.

Thousands of people have been killed, the majority of them civilians, and more than a million others have been forced to flee their homes.

'Ethnic Cleansing'

UN Human Rights Council adopted a resolution that will allow a team to investigate whether war crimes and crimes against humanity are being committed in Iraq.

UN officials continue to gather "strong evidence" that serious violations of international human rights and humanitarian law had been committed in areas under IS control.

UN says Christian, Yazidi, Turkmen, Shabak, Kaka'i, Sabeans and Shia communities had "all been targeted through particularly brutal persecution" and that IS had "ruthlessly carried out what may amount to ethnic and religious cleansing".

"Hundreds of thousands of civilians from these communities have fled to remote and desolate locations where unconfirmed reports indicate that scores of children, elderly people and people with disabilities have been dying as a result of exhaustion and deprivation."

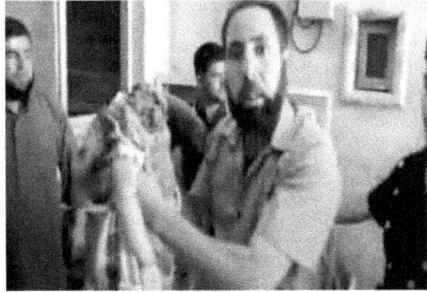

Yazidis have been targeted for extremely harsh treatment. Many men who refused to convert to Islam were reportedly executed, while women and young girls were allotted as slaves to IS fighters. At least 2,250 Yazidi women and children are reportedly being held hostage.

UN says evidence suggested that Iraqi government forces had also killed detainees and shelled civilian areas.

UN received reports of at least 650 male inmates of Badouch Prison in Mosul being shot dead by IS militants on 10 July. Witnesses and survivors said inmates claiming to be Sunni were taken away, while Shia and members of other religious or ethnic communities were ordered into ditches and killed.

Pro-government militiamen were accused of killing worshippers at a Sunni mosque in Diyala province

Shelling and air strikes by Iraqi security forces have also killed and injured many civilians.

Pope Says Violence In Iraq 'Deeply Offends God And Humanity'

Pope Francis said the violence in Iraq - which has included the persecution of Christians - offends God and humanity as he held a silent prayer for victims of the conflict during his weekly address in Rome yesterday.

The Argentinian pontiff said: 'We are left incredulous and dismayed by the news coming from Iraq.

'Thousands of people, among them many Christians, banished brutally from their houses, children dying of hunger and thirst as they flee, women kidnapped, people massacred, violence of all kinds, destruction everywhere

'All of this deeply offends God and deeply offends humanity.'

A hush fell over the crowd in Saint Peter's Square after Francis, who has been tweeting calls to pray for the people of Iraq, interrupted his prepared speech to ask for a moment of silence.

Francis thanked volunteers in Iraq and said his personal envoy Cardinal Fernando Filoni would leave Rome for Iraq today, 'to assure those dear people that I am near them'.

The Vatican added in a statement that the Pope met Filoni to discuss the mission, which is intended to show solidarity with Christians in Iraq in particular, and gave the envoy a sum of money to provide urgent help to the people worst affected.

May be it's time for Pope to understand that "all" violence deeply offends God, whether directed towards humans or animals, it doesn't matter. All are God's children. Our spiritual leaders need to realize that violence inside the slaughterhouses and violence outside are interrelated.

Reference

Angus Martyn, The Right of Self-Defence under International Law-the Response to the Terrorist Attacks of 11 September, Australian Law and Bills Digest Group, Parliament of Australia Web Site, 12 February 2002.

Thalif Deen. "Politics: U.N. Member States Struggle to Define Terrorism", Inter Press Service, 25 July 2005.

Spring Fever: The Illusion of Islamic Democracy, Andrew C. McCarthy - 2013

African Politics: Beyond the Third Wave of Democratisation, Joelien Pretorius - 2008

Hoffman, Bruce (1998). Inside Terrorism. Columbia University Press.

"Inside Terrorism", The New York Times, 3rd January 2004.

Jeffrey (December 2003)."Bounding the Global War on Terrorism". Strategic Studies Institute (SSI).

http://rt.com/news/196512-isis-yazidi-women-slavery/

http://www.cnn.com/2014/10/30/world/meast/isis-female-slaves/

http://www.ibtimes.co.in/isis-news-raped-abused-yazidi-women-beg-west-bomb-their-brothel-kill-them-video-612643

http://www.washingtontimes.com/news/2014/oct/23/yazidi-sex-slave-begs-west-to-bomb-brothel-where-s/

Simon Tomlinson, The Daily Mail, 13 August 2014

24

'Today There Is A Third World War'

Pope Francis Condemns 'Piecemeal' World Of War

A hundred years ago, Giovanni Bergoglio fought in some of the fiercest battles of the First World War.

Luckily he survived, but his grandson Jorge Mario Bergoglio, now Pope Francis, remembers how the old man would only speak of the 'painful memories' of the Great War.

And in September 2013, the pontiff made a holy pilgrimage to Italy's largest war memorial to pay homage to the sacrifices made by Giovanni and millions of others. Standing amid row upon row

of tombstones dedicated to Italian soldiers who fell during the First World War, Francis reiterated his calls for peace among nations amid new threats from the Middle East and Eastern Europe.

He recalled the trauma suffered by his own grandfather, who fought during Italy's bloody campaign along the Isonzo River, close to the graveyard, before emigrating to Argentina after the war.

Between 1915 and 1917 the Italian army launched a series of bloody attacks against the Austro-Hungarian forces stationed along the Isonzo River, losing almost half of all soldiers killed in the conflict there.

The pontiff prayed among gravestones in an Austro-Hungarian cemetery, before visiting Italy's largest war memorial where he held an open-air mass beside a Fascist-era monument to 100,000 fallen soldiers.

"Those who kill animals and give them unnecessary pain—as people do in slaughterhouses—will be killed in a similar way in the next life and in many lives to come. One can never be excused from such an offense. If one kills many thousands of animals in a professional way so that other people can purchase the meat to eat, one must be ready to be killed in a similar way in his next life and in life after life. There are many rascals who violate their own religious principles. According to Judeo-Christian scriptures, it is clearly said, "Thou shalt not kill." Nonetheless, giving all kinds of excuses, even the heads of religions indulge in killing animals while trying to pass as saintly persons. This mockery and hypocrisy in human society bring about unlimited calamities; therefore occasionally there are great wars. Masses of such people go out onto battlefields and kill themselves. Presently they have discovered the atomic bomb, which is simply awaiting wholesale destruction. If people want to be saved from the killing business life after life, they must cease sinful activity. The International Society for Krishna Consciousness recommends that everyone abandon meat-eating, illicit sex, intoxication and gambling. We therefore request everyone to abandon sinful activity and chant the Hare Krsna mantra. In this way people can save themselves from repeated birth and death."

~ Srila Prabhupada, Caitanya-caritamrta, Madyam lila 24:251

Francis' grandfather, Giovanni Bergoglio, was one of thousands of Italians who fought in the trenches near the Isonzo River, which was part of Austria at the time, but now part of Slovenia close to the border with Italy.

'I have heard many painful stories from the lips of my grandfather,' the pope has said.

Hundreds of thousands of Italian troops died trying to cross the Isonzo River between 1915 and 1917.

The elder Bergoglio, who was drafted at age 30 as Italy entered the war, took part in the Isonzo campaign, obtaining a certificate of good conduct and 200 lire at the war's end, according to documents from the time.

With postwar Italy's economy stalled, he emigrated to Argentina where Pope Francis - then known as Jorge Mario Bergoglio - was born.

'The Repiduglia sanctuary until 20 years ago was always full of visitors, but it has been forgotten by institutional memory,' the local Mayor said.

'The papal visit is very important because it renews attention on this history.' The monument consists of 22 granite steps leading upwards to three large crosses. It marks the burial spot of 100,000 Italian soldiers, around 60,00 of which have never been identified.

Blood-Soaked Hills Of The Isonzo: Doomed Attacks That Killed Almost 600,000 Italian Soldiers

When Italy joined the First World War in 1915, one of its first moves was to launch an attack against Austro-Hungarian forces

> *"To be non-violent to human beings and to be a killer or enemy of poor animals is Satan's philosophy. In this age there is always enmity against animals, and therefore the poor creatures are always anxious. The reaction of the poor animals is being forced on human society, and therefore there is always the strain of cold or hot war between men, individually, collectively or nationally...*
>
> *~ Pythagoras*

massing along a mountain range at the head of the Adriatic Sea, in what is modern-day Solvenia.

Italian General Luigi Cadorna believed the best chance of breaking through the defensive line was to cross the north end of the Isonzo River, bypassing the mountains and coming at the Austro-Hungarian forces from the rear.

However, Italy's entrance to the war was well anticipated, and Austria-Hungary had sent large numbers of men and artillery to the region ahead of time which were dug in along mountainous

ridges overlooking key attacking positions.

Modern historians largely accept that there were 12 battles of the Isonzo, though the fighting was so fierce and prolonged that one battle often merged into the next, and the total has long been disputed.

"I am full of the burnt offering of rams and the fat of fed beasts. I delight not in the blood of bullocks, or of lambs, or of goats...Bring no more vain offerings... When you spread forth your hands, I will hide mine eyes though you make many prayers, and I will not hear you. For your hands are full of blood..."
~ Isaiah 1:11-15

Between June 1915 and March 1916, the Italian forces tried to cross the river on five separate occasions, but on every one they were repelled, suffering heavy losses for only modest gains in territory.

During the sixth battle, from August 6–17, 1916, General Cadorna finally captured the town of Gorizia and with it a bridgehead across the Isonzo, which marked the first victories of the campaign.

Fearing that the line was in danger of being overrun, the Germans reinforced their allies and in October 24 their combined forces took to the offensive, forcing the Italians to retreat.

Many war-weary soldiers simply threw down their weapons and were captured, though many units continued to fight as they retreated toward the Piave River where they finally held the line.

In total, between 300,000 and 600,000 troops died during the fighting, almost half of all the Italian soldiers to be killed during the war, making it the worst defeat in the country's military history.

Source

Chris Pleasance, The Daily Mail, 13 September 2014

Catholic News, 9/14/2014

Stefano Rellandini, Reuters September 13, 2014

Tefano Rellandini, Redipuglia Italy, Sep 13, 2014

BBC, 13 September 2014

Dangerously Violent, Trigger-Happy Masses

Woman Kills Three For Last X-Box at Chicago Wal-Mart

A woman was arrested in November 2013 for stabbing to death three shoppers at a Chicago-area Wal-Mart in order to secure the store's last X-Box One.

Mary Robbins, a married mother of two, reportedly wrestled her competitors to the ground before fatally wounding them with a sharpened Phillips head screwdriver.

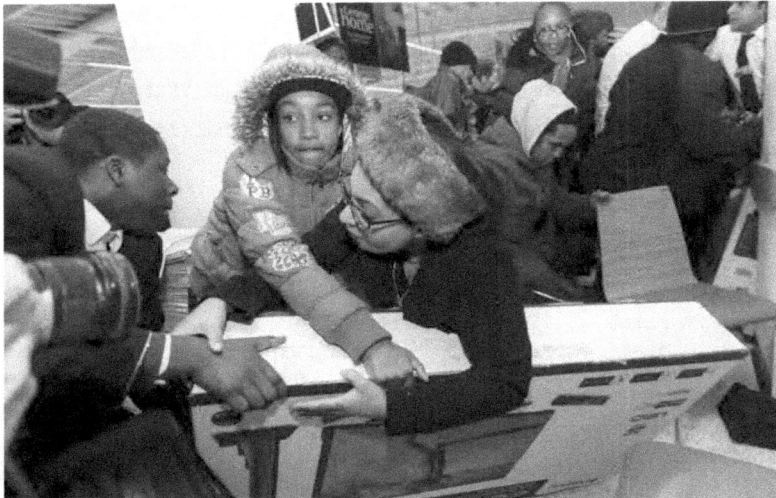

133

The victims are said to include a sociology student at Northwestern University, a chemistry teacher at at local high school and a young pregnant woman buying a system for her brother.

Robbins fled the scene and was apprehended at home hours later after police identified her license plates on the store's surveillance camera. Although many are shocked by the senseless violence, the alleged perpetrator is unrepentant.

"Of course I'd do it all over again," Robbins proclaimed from a Cook County jail cell. "My little Dustin is going to have an X-Box for Christmas this year. No one can take that away from him. Not even the police."

"Shopping isn't a hobby for me, it's a war. So I have to spend a little time behind bars. So what? I didn't punk out. I fought hard for my family, and I'm proud of that."

This incident of shopping violence comes on the heels of what experts are describing as the deadliest Black Friday weekend ever. All across the country people are dying at an increased pace. Every year drastically exceeds previous years death totals for the Holiday season.

"The figures we are looking at this Thanksgiving are incredible unnerving… and this data is just from Thursday night. We only use to have to worry about Friday," said FBI Specialist Harry Carry.

"We had six people trampled to death at the Best buy, four at the Bed Bath Beyond, and two fatal stabbings at Wal-Mart," said Miami police spokesman Sgt. James Loftus.

"Every act of irreverence for life, every act which neglects life, which is indifferent to and wastes life, is a step towards the love of death. This choice man must make at every minute. Never were the consequences of the wrong choice as total and as irreversible as they are today. Never was the warning of the Bible so urgent: "I have put before you life and death, blessing and curse. Choose life, that you and your children may live."
~ Erich Fromm (on Deuteronomy 30:19)

Inside a local Target, the crazed shoppers had lost what was rest of their minds. "We came outside and the Quiznos was burnt to the ground by angry shoppers. I think the Target had ran out of some kind of toaster," said a shopper who wished not to be named because she was supposed to be bailing out her boyfriend who had punched another shopper over a set of soup ladles.

A witness says an old lady beat a kid with her purse in order to get the last toothbrush holder.

"I don't even have real teeth anymore and have no need for such an item but it was over 35 percent off. I might be old but I'm not dumb, of course I will take advantage of that deal," says 88-year-old Margaret Robinson.

According to Wal-Mart, America's largest retailer, the company admits that more than 5,000 shoppers will be killed at their stores this holiday season.

"We include people killed from Thanksgiving to Christmas, so it's not like they are all dying in one day. Besides, more kids will die making this junk than they do buying it, we see that as a positive," Wal-Mart spokesman Charlie Hass said.

I am a Vegetarian. I have 3 Vegetarian children 2-6 years of age. Well mannered, mellow, they've sleep through the night from day one, and when I recovered in 2 weeks after giving birth to the first two and with my last child, on a raw Vegetarian diet I recovered in less than a week! I have been Vegetarian for going on 9 years. I haven't been sick since I've gone Vegetarian. The children have got sick 2-3 times in their lifetime. We drink green smoothies every morning for breakfast. They don't get jealous if I hold another child/baby, instead they cater to them. A book I recommend friendly to all types of healthier eating, The Beauty Detox Solution by Kimberly Snyder CN. I bought her book for everyone I know. Answers ALL your questions about food. IF you want to be successful and stay Vegetarian her book is the one to get, if you want to eat healthier her tips are great! It's a lifestyle and truly the fountain of youth! Everyone deserves to be incredibly healthy, ridiculously gorgeous and glowing in sheer bliss.
~ Danielle, March 19, 2012

One shopper, Sami Zayn, described the day as "chaos" and went on to say, "Thanksgiving used to be about fighting with your family, not other shoppers."

Source

The Daily Currant, Crime, Nov 30, 2013. Even though the article may be a spoof, it captures the spirit of America's consumerism nicely.

The Link

Between Meat Production and Human Rights

There is no doubt that the world is suffering through an environmental crisis. Climate change, deforestation, water scarcity and the state of resources in relation to population growth, are all impacted directly as a result of the farming and consumption of nonhuman animal products.

The world is increasing its overall consumption of meat and seafood (Goodland & Anhang, 2009; World Watch Institute, 2008; McMichael et.al, 2007), and yet there is a food crisis where resources are funnelled into feeding animals so that humans in wealthy countries can consume them (Singer, 2004). This article explores the connections between eating the flesh of animals and environmental destruction which significantly impacts on the rights of every being on the planet.

The world's output of 'meat' has increased up to five times in the second half of the twentieth century (Tudge, 2004, p.1; Worldwatch Institute, 2008, p.10). Over the last seven years, the tonnage of livestock products has increased by twelve percent worldwide (Goodland &

"Nothing will benefit human health and increase chances for survival on Earth as much as the evolution to a vegetarian diet."
~ Albert Einstein (as cited in Marcus, 2001, p.2)

Anhang, 2009). There are now twenty two billion farm animals, which include 15 billion chickens and 1.3 billion cattle.

In Australia, which is a major beef and veal exporter, each person consumed an average of thirty seven kilos of beef per year (ABS, 2005). Tudge estimates that by 2050, the world's livestock population will have grown to the point where the plant food it consumes could feed approximately four billion people, if it wasn't used for meat production (Tudge, 2004, p.1).

The Link Between Human Rights And The Environment

Article 25 of the Universal Declaration of Human Rights (UDHR) states that:

"Everyone has the right to a standard of living adequate for the health and well-being of himself and his family, including food, clothing, housing and medical care ..."

Although contested in many arenas (Zarsky, 2002), the link between human rights and the environment has long been recognised in international law (Sensi, 2007). As recognised by Sensi (2007), pollution of the water and air, loss of biodiversity, desertification and environmental degradation all have a negative impact on human rights (p.27). The Convention on the Rights of the Child (CRC) was the first universal treaty to recognise the dependence on human rights to the state of the environment (Sensi, 2007).

Unfortunately, the only legalised treaties that enshrines the right to a healthy environment is the African Charter and the San Salvador Protocol. However, it is clear to see that a healthy environment is a pre-condition for the enjoyment of many human rights, such as life, health, and wellbeing (Sensi, 2007). Human rights law provides a means to protect the environment against degradation and pollution that have the effect of limiting human rights obligations.

This being so, the impact of killing animals for meat production on environmental degradation is linked to human rights. When a government ratifies a human rights treaty, they are also creating a legal obligation to ensure that the human rights of its citizens are protected. This means doing everything in their power to protect the rights enshrined, such as the health and wellbeing of the country.

Numerous United Nations bodies have underlined this link as imperative to human rights and have reinforced that human rights are interconnected and interrelated (Vienna Declaration and Programme of Action, 1993).

This article is not suggesting that the environment has rights in any sense. However, the rights of living beings, including animals, should be protected overall, and one could argue that the environment is a precondition to enjoying all human rights.

To explore this link further, we will investigate the environmental impacts of animal meat production and consumption in depth.

Facts and Figures: Impact of meat production on the Environment

Atmosphere and Climate Change

Climate change is the most serious challenge facing the human race (Annan, 2005, p.24; Steinfeld et.al, 2006, p.xxi). Climate change impacts the temperature of the Earth, which in-turn impacts on the ice caps, rising sea levels which causes flooding, droughts, shifting currents and weather patterns and endless devastating environmental consequences (Rowlands, 2002; Steinfeld et.al, 2006; McMichael et.al, 2007).

There have been many respected scientific researchers who have explored the link between environmental destruction and

Paramahamsa: They say meat eating is natural....and we give them the argument, could you eat if we brought you the cow and let you kill her yourself, and they say, "No, I could not do that." But yet, when the cow's meat is killed and wrapped up in a nice wrapper, they eat, and they don't have any bad feeling about it.

Prabhupada: This is called maya. He cannot face the actual situation, but, covered by some maya, he accepts. This is another example of maya. Directly killing the animal he cannot tolerate, but when it is covered by maya, the same danger, he accepts.

~ Srila Prabhupada (Morning Walk -- June 13, 1974, Paris)

the production of meat, including the United Nations Food and Agricultural Organisation (FAO).

In 2006, the FAO released a report entitled 'Livestock's Long Shadow' which outlined many concerns in relation to the production and consumption of beef. The research found that the livestock sector accounted for eighteen percent of the world's total greenhouse gas emissions measured in CO_2 equivalent (Steinfeld et.al, 2006, p. xxi). Similarly, McMichael et.al (2007) found that one fifth of the world's greenhouse gas emissions are attributable to agricultural activity, especially livestock production, which is the equivalent of twenty percent of global total emissions (p.1253).

Although there are different numbers ranging from eighteen to twenty two percent, the consensus is that the contribution to global emissions is greater than that of every day transport of everyone on the globe (Ogino et. al., 2007; McMichael et al., 2007; Steinfeld et.al, 2006).

Recently, Goodland and Anhang (2009) concluded that the above figures have been "vastly underestimated", and that the life-cycle and supply chain of domestic animals raised for food account for "at least half of all human-caused GHG's [Greenhouse Gas Emissions]" (p.11).

Based on their analysis, they believe that if we were to adopt a plant based diet devoid of all animal products, we would be able to reverse climate change (Goodland & Anhang, 2009).

Deforestation has also been a consequence of meat production (Goodland and Anhang, 2009). Forests have been destroyed to make way for the grazing of animals to be used for human consumption. Over the past twenty five years, approximately half of Central America's rainforests have been cleared, largely to provide beef to North Americans (Rowlands, 2002).

Deforestation has led to the extinction of species, erosion of topsoil, and flooding. But the most devastating impact of deforestation is the release of massive amounts of carbon into the atmosphere. The livestock sector accounts for nine percent of anthropogenic CO_2 emissions which derives especially from deforestation due to land use changes, such as expansion of pastures or arable land for feedcrops (Steinfeld et. al, 2006).

The livestock sector emits thirty percent of anthropogenic methane, sixty five percent of anthropogenic nitrous oxide, the great majority from manure, and almost two thirds (sixty four percent) of anthropogenic ammonia which contributes to acid rain and acidification of ecosystems (Steinfeld et. al, 2006, p.xxi).

Biodiversity is affected by the expansion of pastures and rangeland degradation attributed to the livestock industry. Overfishing for livestock feed has had a strong impact on the biodiversity of marine ecosystems (FAO, 2006, p.273). Deforestation has also contributed to habitat loss for many species, especially in Latin America. Livestock now occupy vast areas which were once home to wildlife.

Weather plays a major role in the production of food (Davis, 2006). The contribution of pollution from animal products is effecting weather patterns and therefore affecting the right of people to adequate food.

All of these practices which are engaged to produce and rear animals for meat contributes to the intensification of climactic changes and environmental degradation.

A report by Schwartz and Randall (2003) for the Pentagon suggested that global warming proves a greater risk to the world than terrorism and could lead to catastrophic droughts, riots and famines (as cited in Steinfeld et. al, 2006, p.6).

Land Degradation

The farming of animals, especially livestock accounts for twenty six percent of the icefree terrestrial surface of the planet (FAO, 2006; Steinfeld et. al, 2006, p.xxi). One of the biggest problems is the amount of land which is dedicated to feedcrops (FAO, 2006). Presently, the amount of land dedicated to production of food for animals to be killed for human consumption is thirty three percent of total arable land.

As Steinfeld et.al. (2006) point out, all livestock production accounts for seventy percent of all agricultural land and thirty percent of the total land surface on the planet (p.xxi).

About twenty percent of the world's pastures have been degraded, mostly through overgrazing, compaction and erosion created by livestock. Flannery (2005) suggests that the 22 million hectares of arable land in Australia has degraded and is in need of soil restoration (p.367).

Because additional land for cultivation has been severely limited, the future of agricultural production has come and will come from intensification of land that is already cropped or grazed (Steinfeld et. al, 2006, p.5). This being so, the amount of food directly put in to feeding animals for human use needs to be looked at critically.

"Animals that we eat are the nutritional equivalent of middlemen. We put things in protein, carbohydrates, iron, calcium and so on-and we get out a whole lot less than we put in. This means that raising animals for food is an extremely inefficient use of land." (Rowlands, 2002, p.202)

Water

"The water that goes into a 1000 pound steer would float a destroyer." (Newsweek as cited in Rowlands, 2004, p.203)

It is not only land that is used inefficiently for meat production. Fresh water, the ever increasing scarce and depleting resource, is also used to excess for the production of animal products. It is estimated that sixty four percent of the world's population is expected to live in 'water stressed' basins by the year 2025 (Steinfeld et. al, 2006, p.xxii).

This is a very real and urgent problem. The livestock industry has much to answer for considering it uses over eight percent of global human water use, mostly for irrigation of feedcrops.

Singer (2002) has noted that more than half of all water consumed in the United States goes to livestock (p.167). An example to put this into perspective; it takes 500 litres to farm a kilo of potatoes, 900 litres for a kilo of wheat, approximately 2000 for rice or soy beans, 3500 for a single chicken or, 100 000 litres for just one kilo of beef (Tudge, 2004, p.1).

Water pollution due to meat production has also become a serious issue. The major sources of water pollution today are from animal wastes, antibiotics and hormones injected into animals for greater meat production, chemicals from tanneries, fertilisers and pesticides used for feedcrops, and sediments from eroded pastures (Steinfeld et. al, 2006, p.xxii).

In the United States, livestock are responsible for fifty five percent of erosion and sediment, thirty seven percent of pesticide use, fifty percent of antibiotic use, and a third of the loads of nitrogen and phosphorous spilled into freshwater resources (Steinfeld et. al, 2006, p.xxii).

It is not only pollution that causes a detrimental impact on water supplies. Livestock are also responsible for compacting the soil, reducing filtration, degrading the banks of watercourses, and lowering water tables (Steinfeld et. al, 2006, p.xxii). As well as this, deforestation due to meat consumption increases runoff and reduces dry season flows.

Water pollution and ammonia have affected the quality and health of aquatic life (FAO, 2006). The amount of toxins which run into waterways has increased due to non-human animal meat production. Fecal matter and antibiotics find their way into the water where fish are found.

In turn people are eating contaminated fish which causes major health problems. For example, the demand for cheap fish has become an issue for the Togean people whose livelihoods have depended on fishing, but the water is now contaminated by Cyanide due to fishing practices which seek to maximise the catch (Lowe, 2000).

Energy/Resources

Take the case of Australia whose population now sits at 22,038,731 (ABS, 2009). Flannery estimates that Australia only has the capacity to feed between 20-30 million (Flannery, 2005, p.368). One of the reasons for this is that Australian's are so dependent on cattle, sheep and pigs for their meat.

Flannery (2005) has suggested that if Australia wanted to continue to eat 'meat' considering its population demands and environmental sustainability, they would need to start eating kangaroos, goats, feral pigs, rabbits, wild dogs, horses and emus (p.398). Of course, the alternative of a plant based diet sounds like a more advantageous and appealing option for everyone involved.

With the growth of population comes the increased demand for livestock. By 2025, the FAO estimates that the world wide number of livestock will double (Goodland and Anhang, 2009). This of course means an increase in greenhouse gas emissions and environmental destruction.

The amount of energy consumed to produce meat is enormous (Rowlands, 2002). An issue especially pressing, is the energy and resources allocated to factory farming, then slaughter, transporting of carcases and the refrigeration (Goodland & Anhang, 2009). Considering our rapidly depleting reserves of fossil fuels and other natural energy resources, the energy used to produce animal meat could be better managed to minimise environmental impact and maximise healthy food production.

Food Production and Hunger

"... the fundamental right of everyone to be free from hunger ..."
Article 11 (2) of the ICESCR

"It's going to be almost impossible to feed future generations the kind of diet we have now in western Europe and north America."
Anders Berntell from Stockholm Water Institute (as cited in Kirby, 2004)

As Rowlands (2002) puts it, a bull is, in effect, a protein converter (p.201). In 2002, a total of six hundred and seventy million tonnes of cereals were fed to livestock, representing approximately a third of the global cereal harvest (Steinfeld et. al, 2006, p.12).

Another three hundred and fifty million tonnes of protein rich processing byproducts are used as feed, including brans, oilcakes and fishmeal (Steinfeld et. al, 2006, p.12). It takes twenty one pounds of vegetable protein to feed a calf to produce only one pound of animal protein that is then available for humans to eat (Singer, 2002, p.165; Rowlands, 2002, p. 202).

MAKE MEAT ILLEGAL

So for every pound of cattle protein, we could have had twenty one pounds of vegetable protein instead and fed many more people. More than ninety percent of what is put into the bull is lost. Other animals are not quite as 'inefficient', as Rowlands (2002) puts it. Pigs, sheep and chickens work out to be a conversion ratio of around ten to one; that is ten pounds of vegetable protein to every pound of animal flesh (Rowlands, 2002, p.202).

Peter Singer (2003) puts forward this analogy. If we have one acre of land that is used to grow high-protein plant food, such as beans, we will reap between three hundred and five hundred pounds of protein from the acre. Comparatively, the land could be used to grow a crop that will be fed to animals that we feed, and then kill for food. The protein will then be forty to fifty five pounds of protein from the acre (p.165).

Of course protein is not the only nutrient which plants can provide. The total amount of calories produced by plant foods compared to non-human animal foods always shows plant foods to come out on top. For example, one crop of oats or corn produces about twenty times more calories per acre as beef (Singer, 2002, p.166).

Another myth perpetuated by the meat and dairy industry is the amount of iron that meat can provide. An acre of broccoli produces sixteen times the amount of iron as an acre of cattle and five times as much calcium as milk (Singer, 2002, p.166).

"Famines are wars over the right to existence."

(Davis, 1996, p.56)

The point of all of these figures is to demonstrate the amount of food and nutrition that could be going to hungry people compared to feeding animals so we can eat them to satisfy taste rather than nutritional requirements. The fact is, the eating of animal flesh is making some people rich, and causing the suffering of humans and animals everywhere. We are presently in a food crisis (FAO, 2008).

Realistically, stopping meat consumption will not solve the problem of world hunger as there are many political and economic factors involved in this issue. However, stopping the consumption of animal products would be a major step forward, not only to feed hungry people, but also in overcoming unnecessary suffering of animals.

In 1974, a study by Lester Brown of the Overseas

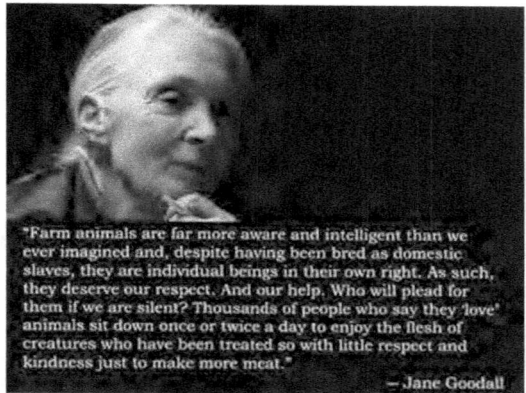

"Farm animals are far more aware and intelligent than we ever imagined and, despite having been bred as domestic slaves, they are individual beings in their own right. As such, they deserve our respect. And our help. Who will plead for them if we are silent? Thousands of people who say they 'love' animals sit down once or twice a day to enjoy the flesh of creatures who have been treated so with little respect and kindness just to make more meat."

— Jane Goodall

Development Council found that if Americans were to reduce their meat consumption by ten percent for only one year, it would mean that there would be at least an extra twelve million tonnes of grain for human consumption (Singer, 2002). This is enough to feed sixty million people!

"Every human being has the inherent right to life."

Article 6, UDHR.

The food wasted due to animal production in affluent nations would be enough to end hunger and malnutrition across the globe (assuming equal distribution) (Singer, 2002, p. 166). There are 923 million people worldwide who are undernourished and 843 million people are living in chronic hunger (FAO, 2008). The World Health Organisation calls malnutrition the 'silent emergency', and says that it contributes to the deaths of at least half of the 10.4 million child deaths that occur every year (Kirby, 2004).

There are many reasons for this, including the rising price of food commodities due to demand for biofuels and the rising price of oil, distribution problems, climate change and changes in agricultural policies of OECD countries. However, even the United Nations FAO attributes part of the problem to livestock production and feedcrops (FAO, 2008). We have no excuse to conveniently put this issue to the side simply because we enjoy the taste of meat. This is a human rights issue. People in other countries are dying from hunger and malnutrition because we prefer to ignore the bad habits of affluent nations.

Davis (1996) discusses the political ecology of famine and points out the link between the politics of wealthy countries that influences the human rights of those in developing countries. What is of particular importance in relation to this article, is the way that the mass production of meat has impacted on the poorest people. The 'meat industry' is run and sustained by wealthy nations whose main objective is to maximise wealth and to satiate wealthy people's taste for flesh.

As this article has indicated, the impact of meat consumption on the environment is devastating. Poverty and famine is just another way that Western countries keep developing countries in a state of political reliance and submission. The millions who die of malnutrition has ultimately been a policy choice by the rich and the powerful (Davis, 1996, p.55). The main losers in the environmental crisis are those from developing nations who do not have the resources to match those in wealthy nations. This in turn impacts on basic human rights.

Conflict

Environmental degradation has been linked with war and conflict. The Southern African Millennium Ecosystem Assessment (Biggs et. al, 2004) discusses the relationship between ecological stress and social conflict.

It suggests that conflict may indeed cause environmental degradation, but it also might trigger a conflict due to competing for dwindling resources such as land for cattle, woodfuel shortages and water scarcity. The report outlines many examples where faction fighting over scarce land for cattle production has led to killings (Biggs et. al, 2004).

Examples were also given where major ecological problems have gone hand in hand with recent violent conflict in the Congo, Burundi and Rwanda.

This connection suggests that the consumption of animal products is connected to human rights issues on many levels and as far reaching as one can possibly imagine. If we take control of environmental degradation, and a good starting point would be slowing down the consumption of meat, the impact around the globe would be phenomenal.

Impact Of Meat Consumption Directly On Human Beings

Health

"... the right of everyone to the enjoyment of the highest attainable standard of physical and mental health ..."
Article 12 (i) of the ICESCR

Environmental degradation impacts the health and wellbeing of all human beings in a number of ways both directly and indirectly (Steinfeld et. al, 2006, p.6). For example, an indirect effect would be the exposure of humans to infectious diseases due to climate change.

Diseases such as Dengue Fever and Malaria are very sensitive to climactic changes as well as Schistosmiasis and Bilharzia which are carried by water snails and affected by changing water flows (Steinfeld et. al, 2006, p.6). The World Resources Report of 1999 emphasises that the burden of these environmental related diseases are borne disproportionately by the poor in both developed and developing nations (Steinfeld et. al, 2006, p.6).

There have been increases of 'diseases of affluence' (Singer, 2003; Marcus, 2001; Ayres, 1999). Worldwide there are approximately 1.1 billion overweight people, matching the number who are malnourished (Singer, 2003).

The China Study was a study which looked at diet and lifestyle in a comprehensive way. Scientists looked at the health and wellbeing of 800 million Chinese citizens. It was then picked up by scientists from England, France and the US. A total of 10,200 people were surveyed about their eating habits, lifestyle, exercise habits etc.

"In America, it took 400 years to convince white people not to own black people. So you can understand why this is taking so long....teaching a human being to be compassionate to a chicken or a cow or a pig is twice as hard but it is possible."

- Gary Yourofsky

There were many striking findings in this study. For example, common cancers tended to occur in more urban areas where more meat, oil and animal protein has been consumed (Marcus, 2001).

Dr Campbell, one of the researchers noted, "the project results also suggest that even small amounts of animal products in the diet produces significant increases in disease." (Campbell as cited in Marcus, 2001, pp.29-30)

The World Health Organisation has found that there is a link between eating animal products and an increase in cancers such as colorectal cancer and breast cancer (Ayres, 1999). Cardiovascular disease, diabetes, high blood pressure and cholesterol are all attributed to eating a diet that is high in animal fats.

Some nutritionists have claimed that most people in wealthy countries don't need as much protein as they are getting from meat, and that it is in fact, contributing to obesity (Ayres, 1999).

With the rise of the mass consumption of meat, the demand to produce bigger animals at a faster rate has seen the introduction of new threats to human health, not to mention the abhorrent suffering of animals.

In a particularly cruel process, the flesh of the animals is now being pumped full of genetically modified organisms, hormones, and antibiotics. The full effects of these new chemicals on humans are yet to be realised.

However, many studies have suggested that hormones, antibiotics and genetically modified foods pose a threat to human health and wellbeing (Directorate General for Heath and Consumers, 1999; Edward, 2008; Grocott, 2003) Antibiotics can cause severe reactions including death.

We are all living beings. We are in different dresses. Just like you are European; you have got a different dress. I am an Indian; I have got a different dress. But dress is not consideration. You are a human being; I am a human being. Similarly, all the living entities, they are dressed in 8,400,000's of dresses. But they are living being. And all the living beings are part and parcel of God.

jalaja nava laksani
sthavara laksa vimsati
krmayo rudra-sankhyakah
paksinam dasa laksanam
trimsal laksani pasavah
catur laksani manusah

There are 900,000 kinds of aquatics, 2,000,000 kinds of trees and plants, 1,100,000 kinds of insects and reptiles, 1,000,000 kinds of birds, 3,000,000 kinds of four-legged beasts, and 400,000 kinds of human species.

—Srila Prabhupada

Also, more resistant forms of viruses are developing which pose a serious threat to humans (Avian Flu).

Wellbeing and Violence

In relation to human wellbeing, both spiritually and physically, philosophers, religious leaders and human rights activists such as Mahatma Gandhi, have argued that refraining from consuming 'meat' contributes to the wellbeing of all beings because of the commitment to peace and non-violence.

The link between violence towards non-human animals and humans is distinct. Studies investigating domestic violence have

IF God DIDn't Want US to Eat HUMans, WHY DID HE MaKE tHEM OUt OF MEat?

shown that there is an overlap between child abuse and animal cruelty (Bailey, 2009). Similarly, a 2005 study found that during adolescence, animal cruelty has been associated with other violent behaviours such as bullying, engaging in violence towards siblings and other antisocial behaviour (Goodney-Lea, 2005).

At the very basic level, killing an animal is a violent act, as it would be killing a human being. The animal cries, is fearful, frets for its loved ones, struggles for survival, and suffered pain before it eventually died.

Although very few of us actually have to kill an animal to eat it, the desensitisation of the killing of other beings, whether human or animal, is of concern. Many philosophers and religious leaders have made this connection. For example, Hinduism is one philosophy that attributes the act of eating of meat to violence. It is believed

"But whence is it that a certain ravenousness and frenzy drives you in these happy days to pollute yourselves with blood, since you have such an abundance of things necessary for your subsistence? Why do you belie the earth as unable to maintain you?"

that the killing of the animal, and way in which the animal died has a direct bearing on ourselves and wellbeing. Hindu's believe that we absorb the 'himsa' or violence and that this in turn affects how we live our lives.

The choice not to partake of animal products results from empathy and compassion towards other beings, and therefore a commitment to non-violence. Non-violent activists work to promote peace and undertake consciousness-raising activities to promote peaceful conflict resolution, justice and equality. For vegetarians, this consciousness extends to non-human animals as well as humans. One could argue that a higher level of wellbeing is reached by not contributing to the pain and suffering of any animal, be it human or non-human.

The Argument For Eating Animal Meat

Some say that eating meat is a natural part of the food chain. However, it seems that the game has been changed with the introduction of factory farming and chemical laden animals that are served on the plates of millions every night. Animals are no longer the free roaming spirits that were hunted during the time of our ancestors. There is no reason why human beings need to consume meat to stay healthy.

On the other hand, there are some isolated communities who have no choice but to eat 'meat' for subsistence. There are many places where access to nutrient rich soil is unavailable to farm grain. Also, the isolation can mean a reliance on crops which are affected by weather patterns, such as drought or flooding. They may have some justification to eat an animal to survive, if they have no other choice. Although, we must reinforce that we do have the resources to distribute plant based food to all of the world's poor.

The point is, the vast majority of us do have the choice in eating a plant based diet.

Some people just plainly like the taste of meat. However, when liking the taste of something causes the immeasurable suffering of people, the environment and animals, can we as a global community sit back and not address the consequences?

If there weren't corporate interests involved in the production of meat products, do you still think that humans would still be consuming as much meat as they presently do considering the impacts? There are many soy based meat alternatives currently on the market that can take the place of meat in any recipe if taste is the only concern.

Conclusion

No matter what our ethics are around eating animals, the impact on the environment is beyond debate. If the environment is affected, so are the human rights of everyone, especially the poor. If we are to ignore the impact of meat production and consumption then we must also ignore the impacts of logging, dams and mining as they also have a direct impact on human rights.

This article has explored some of the many issues surrounding the production and consumption of non human animals. It is beyond question that the atmosphere and climate change, land degradation and water scarcity are all affected due to factory farming practices and the amount of animals produced for human consumption.

Food production and famine is one of the most pressing crisis' in relation to human rights. As aforementioned, there are 923 million people worldwide who are undernourished (FAO, 2008). And the food wasted due to animal production could end hunger and malnutrition across the globe (Singer, 2002, p.166). The inadvertent contribution to conflict in relation to resources must also be addressed, as environmental issues have been linked to conflict and resource wars in developing countries.

To conclude, yes, there is a link between the production and consumption of animals and human rights. The production of animal products is something that must be looked at seriously if we are to tackle environmental problems, and even issues surrounding violence in an holistic sense. What must be reinforced is that this is not just an issue for those who chose to live an 'alternative lifestyle'. This is something that everyone can do to contribute to human rights; and all you have to do is leave one thing off your plate.

(By Aloysia Brooks, Copyright 2009)

References

Annan, K. (2005) In Larger Freedom: Towards Development, Security and Human Rights for All. United Nations: New York.

Australian Bureau of Statistics (ABS) (2005) 'Australia's Beef Cattle Industry' in Year Book Australia. Retrieved 10th October, 2008 from http://www.abs.gov.au/ausstats/abs@.NSF/Previousproducts/1301.0Feature%20A rticle232005?opendocument&tab name=Summary&prodno=1301.0&issue=2005 &num=&view=

Ayres, E. (1999) 'Will We Still Eat Meat?' Time. 8th November, 1999. Retrieved 1st October, 2008 from http://www.time.com/time/printout/0,8816,992523,00.html.

Bailey, D. (2009) 'Humane Link Los Angeles: A Coalition for the Eradication of Violence in Los Angeles.' Dissertation California State University. Retrieved 12th September 2009 from ProQuest Database.

Biggs, R., Bohensky, E., Desankar, P., Fabricious, C., Lynam, T., Misselhorn, A., Musvoto, C., Mutale, M., Scholes, R., Shikongo, S. & van Jaarsveld, A. (2004)\ Nature Supporting People: The Southern African Millennium Ecosystem Assessment. Pretoria. Council for Scientific and Industrial research.

Chalmers, D. (2008) 'Discourse on the Violence of Eating Meat.' University for Peace and Conflict Monitor. October 6, 2008. Retrieved 2nd November, 2009 from http://www.monitor.upeace.org/innerpg.cfm?id_article=549

Davis, M. (1996) 'The Political Ecology of Famine' in Peet, R. & Watts, M. (1996) Liberation Ecologies: Environment, development, social movements. London: Routledge. pp. 48-61.

Director General for Health and Consumers (1999) Growth Hormones in Meat Pose Risk to Consumers - Different Levels of Evidence. Retrieved 12th October, 2008 from http://ec.europa.eu/dgs/health_consumer/library/press/press24_en.html

Edward, F. (2008) Nutrition: The Effects of Genetically Modified Foods. Retrieved 12th October, 2008 from http://www.ghchealth.com/genetically-modified-foods.html

Flannery, T. (2005) The Future Eaters (10th edn.). Reed New Holland: Sydney.

Goodland, R. & Anhang, J. (2009) Livestock and Climate Change. World Watch Magazine. Retrieved 1st November, 2009 from http://www.worldwatch.org/node/6294

Goodney-Lea, S. (2005) 'Guns, Explosives, and Puppy Dog Tails: The Social Function of Animal Cruelty.' Dissertation Indiana University.

Grocott, P. (2003) Beef Antibiotics. Catalyst. Aired 24th July, 2003 on ABC. Transcript retrieved 12th October, 2008 from http://www.abc.net.au/catalyst/stories/s910144.htm

Kirby, A. (2004)"Hungry world must eat less meat". BBC News Online. Retrieved 10th October, 2008 from http://news.bbc.co.uk/1/hi/sci/tech/3559542.stm

Lowe, C. (2000) "Global Markets, Local Injustice in Southeast Asian Seas: The live fish trade and Local Fishers in the Togean Islands of Sulawesi" in Charles Zerner (ed) (2000) People, Plants and Justice: The Politics of Nature Conservation. New York: Columbia University Press. pp.234-256.

Marcus, E. (2001) Vegan: The New Ethics of Eating (2nd edn) McBooks Press: Chicago.

McMichael, A., Powels, J., Butler, C. & Voay, R. (2007) Food, Livestock Production, Energy, Climate Change and Health. The Lancet. 370:1253-63. Retrieved 1st October, 2008 from Expanded Academic Index.

Ogino, A., Orito, H., Shimada, K. & Hirooka, H. (2007) Evaluating Environmental Impacts of the Japanese Beef and Cow-Calf System by the Life Cycle Assessment Method. Animal Science Journal. 78(4). pp.424-432. Retrieved 1st September, 2008 from Wiley Interscience database.

Plutarch (c.46-120) On the Eating of Flesh. Retrieved 13th October, 2008 from http://www.bravebirds.org/plutarch.html

Rowlands, M. (2002) Animals Like Us. Practical Ethics Series. Verso: London.

Sensi, S. (2007) 'Human Rights and the Environment-A Practical Guide for Environmental Activists' in Campese, J, Borrini-Feyerabend, de Cordova, Guigner & Oviedo, G. (eds) (2007) Conservation and Human Rights. Policy Matters. 15. ICUN Commission on Environmental, Economic and Social Policy.

Singer, P. (2002) Animal Liberation (3rd edn). HarperCollins Publishers: New York.

Steinfeld, H., Gerber, P., Wassenaar, T., Castel, V., Rosales, M. & de Haan, C. (2006) Livestock's Long Shadow: Environmental Issues and Options. United Nations Food and Agricultural Organisation (FAO). Retrieved 1st October, 2008 from FAO website www.fao.org.

Tudge, C. (2004) "It's a Meat Market: Global Meat Consumption is Increasing Rapidly. Beware, warns Colin Tudge. It's Bad for the Environment and Bad for Us". New Scientist. 19(1). March 13th, 2004. Retrieved 5th October, 2008 from Expanded Academic Index.

United Nations Food and Agricultural Organisation (FAO) (2008) World Food Situation. Retrieved 6th September, 2008 from http://www.fao.org/worldfoodsituation/ wfshome/ en/

Worldwatch Institute (2008) State of the World: Innovations for a Sustainable Economy. Retrieved 14th October, 2008 from ICUN website, http://cmsdata.iucn.org/ downloads/sow_brief_series_lo_res_1.pdf

Zarsky, L. (ed)(2002) Human Rights and the Environment: Conflicts and Norms in a Globalising World. Earthscan: London.

The World

In Need Of Real Civilization

These are excerpts from a conversation between His Divine Grace A.C.Bhaktivedanta Swami Prabhupada and his disciples, recorded in June 1974, in Valencey, France.

In India, the farmers do not even prohibit the monkeys--"All right, let them come in. After all, it is God's property." This is the Krsna conscious system: If an animal, say a monkey, comes to your garden to eat, don't prohibit him. He is also part and parcel of Krsna. If you prohibit him, where will he eat?

I have another story; this one was told by my father. My father's elder brother was running a cloth shop. Before closing the shop my uncle would put out a basin filled with rice. Of course, as in any village, there were rats. But the rats would take the rice and not cut even a single cloth. Cloth is very costly. If even one cloth had been cut by a rat, then it would have been a great loss. So with a few pennies' worth of rice, he saved many dollars' worth of cloth. This Krsna culture is practical. "They are also part and parcel of God. Give them food. They'll not create any disturbance. Give them food."

Everyone has an obligation to feed whoever is hungry--even if it is a tiger. Once a certain spiritual teacher was living in the jungle. His disciples knew, "The tigers will never come and disturb us, because

157

our teacher keeps some milk a little distance from the asrama, and the tigers come and drink and go away."

The teacher would call, "You! Tiger! You can come and take your milk here!" [Laughter.] And they would come and take the milk and go away. And they would never attack any members of the asrama. The teacher would say, "They are my men--don't harm them."

I remember seeing at the World's Fair that a man had trained a lion. And the man was playing with that lion just like one plays with a dog. These animals can understand, "This man loves me. He gives me food; he is my friend." They also appreciate.

When Haridasa Thakura was living in a cave and chanting Hare Krsna, a big snake who also lived there decided to go away. The snake knew--"He's a saintly person. He should not be disturbed. Let me go away." And from Bhagavad-gita we understand, isvarah sarva-bhutanam hrd-dese--Krsna is in every-one's heart, and He is dictating. So Krsna can dictate peace and harmony to the animals, to the serpent, to everyone. [Srila Prabhupada pauses reflectively.]

The Vedic culture offers so many nice, delicious foods, and mostly they are made with milk products. But these so-called civilized people--they do not know. They kill the cows and throw the milk away to the hogs, and they are proud of their civilization--like jackals and vultures. Actually, this Krsna consciousness movement will transform the uncivilized people and bring the whole world to real civilization."

~ Srila Prabhupada (Conversation - Valencey, France, June 1974)

28

"Do Unto Others ..."

This same instruction is present in all religious teachings. The Bible emphatically states, "Thou shall not kill," and Lord Jesus Christ, who always displayed deep compassion for all living beings, stated, "Do unto others as you would have them do unto you." Lord Buddha also taught the principle of ahimsa, nonviolence, specifically to protect innocent creatures from being slaughtered.

People who find that personally killing an animal is too gruesome tend to believe that merely eating flesh does not implicate them in violence. But this opinion is shortsighted and unsupported by any valid spiritual authority. According to the law of karma, all those who are connected to the killing of an animal are liable - the person who gives permission for the killing, the person who kills, the person who helps, the person who purchases the meat, the person who cooks the flesh, and the person who eats it. (These six guilty parties are enumerated in the Manu-samhita, ancient India's book of civic and religious codes.) In a court of law all those who conspire in a murder are considered responsible, especially the party who purchases the assassin's services.

Psychological and emotional growth are essential to a progressive life, and all our thoughts and actions influence our character development. The Bible explains, "As you sow, so shall you reap." And the subtle laws of karma inform us that negative personality traits such as hostility, cruelty, depression, arrogance, apathy, insensitivity, anxiety, and envy are the psychological harvest of those who directly or indirectly make killing a regular feature in their life. When someone adopts a vegetarian diet, it is much easier for him to remain peaceful, happy, productive, and concerned for the welfare of others. As the brilliant physicist Albert Einstein said, "The vegetarian manner of living, by it's purely physical effect on the human temperament, would most beneficially influence the lot of mankind." But when human consciousness is polluted by the effects of the negative karma resulting from destructive and injurious actions, its good qualities become covered.

"Be kind to all kinds, not just humankind."

29

How Can There Be Peace?

This exchange between His Divine Grace A.C. Bhaktivedanta Swami Prabhupada and some of his disciples took place in Geneva, Switzerland, on June 2, 1974.

Disciple: Srila Prabhupada, in a recent study by U.S. agricultural officials, they found that it's uneconomical to eat meat. It takes so much energy and man hours to raise and transport and slaughter the cows that it's very wasteful.

Srila Prabhupada: Wasteful, yes. Therefore I say they have no brain. They are all rascals. Rascal leaders. A little labor in agriculture will be sufficient to produce the family's food stock for the whole year. You work only three months, and you get sufficient food for your whole family. And in the remaining nine months, you chant Hare Krsna.

But these rascals will not do that. They will work hard like asses simply for eating. Nunam pramattah kurute vikarma yad indriya-pritaya aprnoti. They will not accept an easy life.

Disciple: In that agricultural report it said that if people were to eat all the grains they give to the cows and animals, they could get twenty times more calories than by eating meat.

Srila Prabhupada: Yes. Wrong civilization, rascal civilization. And this is due to this rascaldom called nationalism -- "This is my

land." At any moment a person will be kicked out by death, but still
he claims, "It is my land." Janasya moho 'yam aham mameti. This
is the illusion. Nothing belongs to him; still he is fighting, "This is
mine. This is mine." "I" and "mine" -- identifying oneself with the
body and wrongly conceiving that "This is mine." This is the basic
principle of a wrong civilization. Nothing belongs to us. I have come
here to Switzerland. Suppose I remain here for one month and I
claim, "Oh, this is mine." What is this?

So, similarly, we come to this world as guests. We come to the womb of a mother and live here for seventy years or so. And we claim, "This is my land." But when did it become yours? The land was there long,

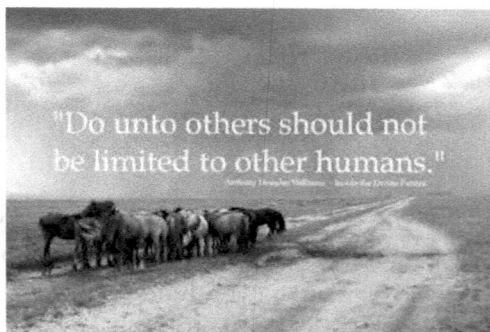

"Do unto others should not be limited to other humans."

long before your birth. How has it become yours? But people have
no sense. "It is mine -- my land, my nation, my family, my society."
In this way, they are wasting time.

These things have been introduced by Western civilization. In
the Vedic civilization there is no such thing as nationalism. You
won't find it there. Have you seen the word "nationalism" in the
Bhagavad-gita? No such thing.

Nationalism is the idea of tribes. In Africa there are still groups
of tribes. Nationalism is the most crude idea of civilization. It is
nothing but developed tribalism. Modern man is not advanced in
civilization. This nationalism is another form of tribalism, that's all.

Disciple: Today, so-called civilized people are actually just
cannibals because they maintain themselves on eating the cow.

Srila Prabhupada: Yes. And they are suffering. Therefore you'll
find that in recent history, every twenty-five years there is a big

war with mass slaughter of people. Nature does not tolerate animal slaughter.

Now India has learned to slaughter animals, imitating the Western countries. And now there is war between India and Pakistan. During two wars between Pakistan and Hindustan, millions of people were killed unnecessarily, without any gain.

Disciple: Just recently India exploded an atomic bomb, and now Pakistan is hurrying to get an atomic bomb also.

Srila Prabhupada: Yes.

This is going on.

Disciple: The Indian government promised that nuclear energy would be only for peaceful purposes.

Srila Prabhupada: No, what do they know about peaceful conditions? They are all rascals. They do not know what a peaceful condition is. The actual peaceful condition is described in the Bhagavad-gita:

bhoktaram yajna-tapasam

sarva-loka-mahesvaram

suhrdam sarva-bhutanam

jnatva mam santim rcchati

"A person in full consciousness of Me [Krsna], knowing Me to be the ultimate beneficiary of all sacrifices and austerities, the Supreme Lord of all planets and demigods, and the benefactor and well-wisher of all living entities, attains peace from the pangs of material miseries."

This is peace. Unless there is Krsna consciousness, where is peace? There cannot be peace. All rascaldom. Na mam duskrtino mudhah prapadyante naradhamah. These rascals and fools -- mayayapahrta-jnana -- have lost all knowledge. How can there be peace? Their endeavors for peace are all useless.

Time Has Come!

March to Close All Slaughterhouses

It is now time to demand, loud and clear, the end of animal slavery and the abolition of all practices that cause them the most harm: breeding, fishing and slaughter.

Saturday, June 14, 2014, was part of a historic international day to denounce the injustice done to all nonhuman victims of human oppression and exploitation. Thousands of poeple joined in a peaceful march through the streets of Sydney, Paris, Toulouse, Toronto, Montreal, Ottawa, New York, Los Angeles, Sydney, Berne, London, Rio De Janeiro and many many other cities to close down all slaughterhouses.

Compassionate citizens are mobilizing to engage communities in the Meat Abolition movement, to end the violence that we inflict on non-human animals.

As a society, we have marched against sexism, racism, and

homophobia. Now, it's time to march against another oppression: speciesism. Our fellow non-human earthlings desperately need us to act against their continuous pain and suffering at the hands of a meat-eating society. Meat consumption causes more suffering and death than any other human activity and is completely unnecessary.

Earthlings changed my life forever.

I had always thought of myself as an animal lover.. I had rescued sick and injured animals all my life, and yet Earthlings proved me to be a hypocrite, I went Vegetarian the very next day and have never looked back, I have met the most amazing people in my new journey, I see animals in a new light .. they are fellow earthlings equal to us, and in many ways better than us.

Where I used to see meat in supermarkets as something to have for my dinner, I now see rows and rows of slaughtered animals and it offends me.

I am not religious or spiritual but I feel reborn or maybe evolved is a better word .. yes I am now vegetarian, my one regret is that I hadn't done it many, many years ago.

~ Lisa Collins, August 17, 2009

It is estimated that every year 1,000 billion aquatic animals are killed worldwide. That's 1,902,588 every minute or 31,710 every second. And, even worse, it's estimated that each year 64 billion land animals are killed worldwide for the appetite of humans. (Or 121,766 every minute and 2,029 every second).

It's time to state clearly the necessity to abolish non-human slavery, and oppose the practices that exploit, torture, and murder them. Please speak out on behalf of those who cannot speak for themselves. This march is part of a movement needed to permanently shut down all slaughterhouses and will ultimately awaken the greatest transformation that humankind has ever known.

Reference

The Scavenger, Why a march to close all slaughterhouses?, 17 June 2014

http://fermons-les-abattoirs.org/

http://www.mtcas.org/

THE AUTHOR

Dr. Sahadeva dasa (Sanjay Shah) is a monk in vaisnava tradition. His areas of work include research in Vedic and contemporary thought, Corporate and educational training, social work and counselling, travelling, writing books and of course, practicing spiritual life and spreading awareness about the same.

He is also an accomplished musician, composer, singer, instruments player and sound engineer. He has more than a dozen albums to his credit so far. (SoulMelodies.com)

His varied interests include alternative holistic living, Vedic studies, social criticism, environment, linguistics, history, art & crafts, nature studies, web technologies etc.

Many of his books have been acclaimed internationally and translated in other languages.

By The Same Author

Oil–Final Countdown To A Global Crisis And Its Solutions

End of Modern Civilization And Alternative Future

To Kill Cow Means To End Human Civilization

Cow And Humanity – Made For Each Other

Cows Are Cool – Love 'Em!

Let's Be Friends – A Curious, Calm Cow

Wondrous Glories of Vraja

We Feel Just Like You Do

Tsunami Of Diseases Headed Our Way – Know Your Food Before Time Runs Out

Cow Killing And Beef Export – The Master Plan To Turn India Into A Desert

Capitalism Communism And Cowism – A New Economics For The 21st Century

Noble Cow – Munching Grass, Looking Curious And Just Hanging Around

World – Through The Eyes Of Scriptures

To Save Time Is To Lengthen Life

Life Is Nothing But Time – Time Is Life, Life Is Time

Lost Time Is Never Found Again

Spare Us Some Carcasses – An Appeal From The Vultures

An Inch of Time Can Not Be Bought With A Mile of Gold

Cow Dung For Food Security And Survival of Human Race

Cow Dung – A Down To Earth Solution To Global Warming And Climate Change

Career Women – The Violence of Modern Jobs And The Lost Art of Home Making

Working Moms And Rise of A Lost Generation

Glories of Thy Wondrous Name

India A World Leader in Cow Killing And Beef Export – An Italian Did It In 10 Years

As Long As There Are Slaughterhouses, There Will Be Wars

Peak Soil – Industrial Civilization, On The Verge of Eating Itself

Corporatocracy : The New Gods – Greedy, Ruthless And Reckless

(More information on availability on DrDasa.com)

www.ingramcontent.com/pod-product-compliance
Lightning Source LLC
Chambersburg PA
CBHW060456280326
41933CB00014B/2767